WITHDRAWN

GIRLS WHO DID

GIRLS WHO DID

Stories of real girls and their careers

BY

HELEN FERRIS

and

VIRGINIA MOORE

Illustrated by

HARRIET MONCURE

NEW YORK
E. P. DUTTON & CO., INC.

THE GIRLS WHOSE STORIES ARE TOLD IN THIS BOOK

And what they are doing now

PAGE

I. GERTRUDE HAWLEY
A GIRL WHO LIKED SPORTS AND WHO HAS BECOME
DIRECTOR OF PHYSICAL EDUCATION IN NORTHWESTERN
UNIVERSITY, EVANSTON, ILLINOIS 3

II. MARION DURELL
A GIRL WHO DIDN'T KNOW SHE WISHED TO BE A
NURSE AND WHO HAS BECOME
DIRECTOR OF NURSES IN THE CITY HOSPITAL, NEW
YORK 21

III. ANNE CARROLL MOORE
A GIRL WHO LOVED BOOKS AND CHILDREN AND
WHO HAS BECOME
HEAD OF THE CHILDREN'S DEPARTMENT OF THE NEW
YORK CITY PUBLIC LIBRARY 35

IV. ETHEL BARRYMORE
A GIRL WHO WAS ALWAYS SURROUNDED BY THE ATMOS-
PHERE OF THE STAGE AND WHO HAS BECOME
AN EMINENT AMERICAN ACTRESS 49

v

PAGE

V. MABEL E. STEWART

A GIRL WHO HAD NO SPECIAL TALENT BUT WHO HAD
TO GO TO WORK AND WHO HAS BECOME
PRIVATE SECRETARY TO THE CHAIRMAN OF THE BOARD
OF DIRECTORS AMERICAN EXCHANGE IRVING TRUST
COMPANY 63

VI. INEZ HAYNES IRWIN

A GIRL WHO ALWAYS LIKED TO WRITE AND WHO
HAS BECOME
AN EMINENT AMERICAN AUTHOR.................. 77

VII. MINNA HALL CAROTHERS

A GIRL WHO ONLY GRADUALLY DISCOVERED WHAT
SHE MOST WISHED TO DO AND WHO HAS BECOME
PRESIDENT OF THE FEDERATION OF ADVERTISING
WOMEN'S CLUBS 93

VIII. NEYSA McMEIN

A GIRL WHO LIKED TO DRAW AND PAINT AND
WHO HAS BECOME
A FAMOUS MAGAZINE ILLUSTRATOR AND PORTRAIT
PAINTER 107

IX. CHARLOTTE COWDREY BROWN

A GIRL WHO LOVED GROWING THINGS AND
WHO HAS BECOME
A GARDENER AND A LECTURER ON GARDENS........ 119

X. EDNA WATSON BAILEY

A GIRL WHO CHOSE TEACHING FIRST OF ALL
AND WHO HAS BECOME
THE HEAD OF THE DEPARTMENT OF SCIENCES IN THE
UNIVERSITY HIGH SCHOOL, UNIVERSITY OF
CALIFORNIA 133

Contents

PAGE

XI. MARION SPRAGUE GILMORE

A GIRL WHO STARTED TO BE A SINGER AND
WHO HAS BECOME

EXECUTIVE DIETITIAN IN THE PENNSYLVANIA HOTEL
IN NEW YORK CITY 153

XII. PEGGY HOYT

A GIRL WHO HAD A KNACK WITH CLOTHES AND
WHO HAS BECOME

A DISTINGUISHED AMERICAN DESIGNER 167

XIII. JEAN NORRIS

A GIRL WHO COURAGEOUSLY ENTERED A FIELD MEN
SAID BELONGED TO THEM AND WHO HAS BECOME

THE FIRST WOMAN JUDGE IN THE STATE OF NEW
YORK 181

XIV. CLARA SIPPRELL

A GIRL WHOSE BROTHER WAS A PHOTOGRAPHER AND
WHO LIKED TO TAKE PICTURES HERSELF AND
WHO HAS BECOME

A DISTINGUISHED AMERICAN PHOTOGRAPHER........ 199

XV. MARGARET E. MALTBY

A GIRL WHO ALWAYS ASKED, 'WHY?' AND
WHO HAS BECOME

AN ASSOCIATE PROFESSOR OF PHYSICS AT BARNARD
COLLEGE, COLUMBIA UNIVERSITY 213

XVI. BRENDA PUTNAM

A GIRL WHO DECLARED, AT TWELVE, THAT SHE
WANTED TO BE A SCULPTOR AND WHO HAS BECOME

AN EMINENT AMERICAN SCULPTOR 229

PAGE

XVII. ALICE FOOTE MacDOUGALL
A GIRL WHO WAS A DÉBUTANTE AND WHO NEVER
EXPECTED TO ENTER BUSINESS AND WHO HAS BECOME
A DEALER IN WHOLESALE ROASTED COFFEE AND
OWNER OF FOUR RESTAURANTS................. 239

XVIII. MARY KINGSBURY SIMKHOVITCH
A GIRL WHO LIKES FOLKS—AND MUSIC—AND BOOKS
AND WHO HAS BECOME
DIRECTOR OF GREENWICH HOUSE, NEW YORK CITY.. 253

XIX. MARIA JERITZA
A GIRL WHO COULD SING BUT WHO WAS VERY SHY
AND WHO HAS BECOME
A DISTINGUISHED INTERNATIONAL MUSICIAN....... 273

XX. YOU
A GIRL WHO IS WONDERING ABOUT HERSELF..... 289

GERTRUDE HAWLEY

A girl
who liked
sports

GERTRUDE HAWLEY

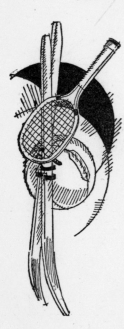

IT was on the college tennis courts.

The deciding match for the championship was about to be played and all the college was out to see. Seniors and Sophomores, Juniors and Freshmen — Odds and Evens — were massed on opposite sides of the court according to the age-old custom of Vassar. Cheers, songs, laughter, rivalry flung, gaily defiant, across white lines and smooth surfaces— then, silence. For two girls in white appeared upon the court, one of whom would that night be tennis champion of the college, privileged to wear the coveted gray sweater with its rose V.

The umpire tossed for courts. The girls shook hands across the net.

"Ready?"

"Serve!"

The match was on. Swift, clean-cut strokes sent the ball whizzing over the net. Fiercely the umpire concentrated upon each play, for these points were being decided not by feet but by inches. It was an evenly-drawn battle, well worth the absorbed attention of the entire college, including the faculty.

But slowly the slim, lithe girl with the straight dark hair parted in the middle began to gain against her taller opponent on the other side of the net. Her playing was not spectacular but it was very sure. She made few sudden dashes across the court. Indeed, there were times when she seemed scarcely to move. Yet, when a ball was shot to the farthest corner, she was there to return it. Back of her keen dark eyes seemed to lurk an uncanny knowledge of where her opponent would place the next shot. And when she made her return, it was with a finished stroke which told of many hours on the tennis court before she came to Vassar. For such tennis is not learned over-night.

"Game — set — match," called the Umpire. "Gertrude Hawley——"

But what she intended to announce about Gertrude Hawley was lost in sudden tumultuous cheering. The college tennis champion and the runner-up shook hands. Crowding friends pulled a gray sweater with bright rose V over Gertrude Hawley's head. Her class burst into triumphant

cheers, followed by a song. The college took up
the refrain zestfully—for what is mere class rivalry when such tennis has been played?

"Oh, Gertrude Hawley
She plays tennis . . ."

Back of the tennis banner, Gertrude and her
class led off the procession. The other classes
fell into line. Singing, they marched across cam-
pus to the class tree, there to wind the newly-won
banner around the sturdy trunk, reminder to all
passers-by that——

"Gertrude Hawley
She plays tennis . . ."

It was another day, years later. I, who had been
among that excited college crowd, was now on my
way to meet Gertrude Hawley, to talk with her
of the years since we both had left Vassar. As I
walked, I thought of that tennis match. Gertrude
Hawley of Vassar days—and now she was head
of the physical education department of a great
university—Northwestern in Evanston, Illinois.
How simple deciding what she would do after
college must have been for her. She had loved
sports—what else had there been for her but to
go where she could direct other girls in their
swimming, their basket-ball, their hockey and
their gymnasium?

"Why, I could write about Gertrude and how

she came to be doing what she is, without asking
her one question!" I thought.

She met me in the candle-lighted room where
we were to have tea, coming toward me with the
same quiet sureness of movement which I had
known so well in our college days together. Her
dark eyes glowed with the same strength. She
took my hand with a grasp that was firm.

And she had a tennis racquet under her arm.

"Of course!" I cried. "You *would* have that.
But you are sailing for Europe early tomorrow
morning. And it's late afternoon now. When—?"

"We'll be stopping in lots of places where
there will be tennis courts," she explained, "so I
had my racquet restrung. There is nothing like
a good game of tennis to set you up for mountain
climbing."

For a few moments our talk wandered over the
years during which we had not seen each other.
Where was Margaret? Barbara? The others?
What were they doing? Were they coming to
next reunion?

And then—"Of course I am not in the least
surprised that you are in Northwestern in charge
of the girls' athletics," I said. "You were planning to do something of the kind all the time you
were in Vassar, weren't you?"

Gertrude Hawley smiled and shook her head.
"My, no. I was far more aimless than that. Oh,
of course I took it for granted that I would do

something after I graduated. But that time always seemed ages away. As for sitting down solemnly and deciding on a career for myself—no, I must be honest. I didn't even think of it. Why, it wasn't until my junior year that I specialized in any of my courses. The faculty must have thought me a veritable drifter!

"But you are right that I have always loved sports," she continued, reminiscently. "As far back as I can remember my family spent summers at Chautauqua. And when I was quite young we decided to remain there the year round. Then for four glorious years I had real winter as well as summer, right outside our door."

And she told me the story of a joyous girlhood. This little girl—she frankly admitted it—was a tomboy. The child was no sooner in the front door than she was out the back, running like a little wild rabbit where little wild rabbits go. She wasn't content with ordinary games like "Piggle" or "Run, sheep, run" or "Follow the leader." In summer she rode her "bike," boy fashion. In winter she strapped on her skates and fastened to her shoulder-blades an impromptu sail rigged out of barb-wire and an old piece of canvas. But tobogganing—that was the most desperate and the most glorious! Again and again, on starry nights, she shot down a snow hill, a streak in the moonlight. And when she reached the bottom, she "hitched." And always, with the first thawing and drying days of spring, there was Gertrude Hawley out on the tennis court, raking the ground smooth, rolling it hard, and chalking off the straight white lines.

As she told me of it, my shoulders squared themselves there in the candle-lighted room. I took a deep, exhilarated breath. For I felt the emanation of strength which issued, somehow, from her fully-alive body. And I knew that her days with the girls of Northwestern are giving her as much as those days on snow-white hills gave little Gertrude Hawley—as much, indeed, as she herself is giving to her girls. Her clear complexion said so and her glowing eyes.

"But don't think an outdoor girl can't love to read, too," continued Gertrude Hawley. "I did. As a child I wanted to read everything and to play everything. And I still do.

"It was the same way at Vassar. I enjoyed my studies. But at the same time I was too interested in what was going on around me to settle down, to specialize, as they say. Yes, books were an adventure to me. But knowing all kinds of girls was an adventure, too, as well as the college athletics. So it wasn't until my third year that I decided the sciences appealed to me just a little more than any of my other courses and I began to specialize in chemistry. By the end of my senior year I was deep in test-tubes and experiments. So when I graduated, I just naturally went into something where my chemistry would be useful to me.

"For four years, then, I worked in the research department of the General Electric Company in Cleveland, analyzing tungsten lamps."

Her brown eyes were bright with the memory of it.

"You liked it, didn't you?" I commented.

"Indeed I did. Those days in that laboratory were really quite thrilling. You see, the consulting chemist of the company, who was in charge, was working to find a platinum substitute. And he did! If you don't enjoy experimenting in a laboratory——"

"I don't," I murmured emphatically — unnoticed.

"You won't understand the excitement of working day after day to find an unknown something you feel sure exists, and discovering it, in the end. Yes, I enjoyed those four years. And then there were my vacations in the White Mountains, up Mount Washington—out in the Yosemite, in California and up more mountains. But——"

"Yes, but?" I ventured.

"There came a time when I realized that I had gone as far as I could in that line of work, without taking more training. I looked around me and saw that the young women who were occupying the more important and more interesting positions of the laboratory were those who had had more scientific training than I, training which it was impossible to get while I was concentrating day after day on experiments. I knew then that it would be necessary for me to spend a year studying—or more, if I wished to go ahead in that field. Fortunately, I had saved enough money to do this if I wished. And yet——"

She paused.

"I wasn't quite sure that I did wish it. Laboratory work is confining. I had not been entirely well since I had undertaken it. Was it sensible, I asked myself, to take training for work which I might be forced to drop in a short while? But if I didn't go on in this, what would I do?

"Just then, K. Forbes came through Cleveland. You remember K., don't you?"

Did I? Does one forget the captain of the hockey team in the class just ahead of hers? Does one forget a president of the athletic association?

"Well, K. had gone on to the physical education course at Wellesley after leaving Vassar, and she was full of enthusiasm for that work. She had always insisted that my natural bent was physical education. I had as regularly replied that sports were my recreation and I didn't intend spoiling them for myself by making them my job.

"This time she found me in an uncertain frame

of mind. I admitted my doubts about laboratory work for me. Yet I was by no means as sure as she about the physical education idea which she again urged upon me. In many ways it appealed to me tremendously. And yet—and yet——

"In the end, I compromised about what to do next. You see, I told you I have always been the kind of person who comes to her decisions gradually."

"Except on the tennis court," I said.

She ignored my interruption. "So I went to Wellesley the next year, taking some courses in the chemistry department and some in the physical education department, much to Katherine's delight. I was trying myself out in both fields. And at the end of the first year I had decided in favor of physical education—chiefly, I think, because I had discovered that you need not draw a hard and fast line between your work and your play. A momentous discovery which almost anyone would have made long before.

"So I completed the course in physical education at Wellesley and accepted a position at Northwestern University where I have been ever since."

And she told me of her work as head of the department of physical education. "Not only is the gymnasium and the class work under our direction," she explained, "but the sports and the individual physical examinations, as well. Our aim is a game for every girl, something she enjoys so much that she forgets it is 'required' and plays it for the sheer fun of it. Whatever the game, we encourage each girl who enters it to play her level best, not to strain herself to do more than that best, nor to content herself with less. If she has it in her to become a champion, she may do so. But we don't want our girls to miss the fun of sports because they can't all be champions. A game for every girl—that is what counts, to my mind."

The result is a full athletic schedule for the girls of Northwestern University. "Take your choice," says Gertrude Hawley to them. "Basketball, tennis, swimming, Indian clubs, pyramid building, indoor baseball, outdoor baseball, archery, track, deck shuffle, dart throwing, quoits, javelin throwing, hockey, clogging, barefoot dancing, folk dancing, aesthetic dancing."

Can't you see the girls of Northwestern, running pellmell down the hockey field, dancing with green grass under the soles of their feet, floating in their swimming pool, speeding an arrow into the bull's eye? The body rejoices to give itself over, entire, to water, wind and sky. Eagerly it throws off the lethargy of study hall and class room for the freer existence of the athletic field and the gymnasium. A girl who has never run until she's breathless has never lived to the utmost.

Gertrude Hawley does not speak second-hand about the pleasures of sports and exercise. She knows them herself, has always known them. And her work to her means giving girls an opportunity to share her delight and to develop bodies that are strong.

"But to me there is more in athletics—in all physical education—than the joy of it," she went on. "There is more even than health, important as that is. There are sportsmanship, fair play and cooperation. The girl who has learned these in her sports is better prepared for whatever she wishes to do. I like to think that our girls go from the basketball court with something very real to help them in their other college activities and in their life after college, too.

"This is one further reason for my interest in the field of physical education. If I make the most of my opportunity, I can do more than give our girls games which they will enjoy. I can do even more than study each girl, developing her by means of diet and exercise to her highest physical capacity. I can link up her sports with all her living."

"Just what do you do at the university?" I asked her.

"Since I have been there, I have done work similar to that which most gymnasium teachers do, later becoming an executive with assistants. At first, I was the only one in the department.

I not only planned the gymnasium classes, the sports and the individual examinations and exercises, I did the teaching, coaching and examining. Later, as the interest of the girls grew, it was necessary to add others to the staff.

"Today, an appreciable part of my time is given to supervising the work, although I still have some classes and coaching. The head of a physical education department is not only responsible for creating new plans, she must see that the work already undertaken is effectively carried out. All classes and games must be well conducted. Each individual girl must be watched so that her sports and her exercises and her diet may be suited to her needs. This takes many hours of careful examining and record-keeping. The head of the physical education department must see that nothing essential is neglected.

"You will be interested to know that many of the girls who have specialized in our department have gone out into the work themselves. For there are splendid opportunities in this field. In fact, it has been my experience that girls who take training for a physical education certificate in a school of recognized merit rarely lack a position. The openings are many because people are recognizing as never before the importance of physical health and development."

"Where are these openings?" I asked Gertrude Hawley.

"Everywhere! In large public schools, in private schools, in normal schools, colleges and universities, on playgrounds, in Y. W. C. A.'s and other organizations and in summer camps. Specialists in folk dancing or gymnastics or swimming often conduct their own private classes. But most of the positions—in fact, all positions of importance—are open only to those who have had training in a recognized school of physical education.

"So the girl who is strong, who loves sports and to whom the idea of directing others in them appeals, will do well to consider this matter of training. Colleges and universities in various parts of the country offer these courses in physical education, as do some teachers' colleges, normal schools and special schools. Any girl who is interested can write to her state university for information or talk with her own gymnasium teacher about it.

"If a girl can afford to attend college, possibly combining her general college course with her training in physical education, I would advise her to do so. Perhaps this is because I am so constantly grateful for my own years at Vassar. Life is more interesting and significant to me because of those years. And even though my studies there did not apparently lead to what I am now doing, they are of more use to me than is at first evident. I feel there is nothing I studied at college, nothing I lived at college which is not in some way helping me today.

"Even my chemistry courses and my later experience in that field were part of my training. I learned to work for facts, to study until I had ascertained them. And now, when I am working with a girl who has some special physical handicap, I apply that same scientific method in my examinations before I make recommendations for her.

"But I wouldn't have you think," concluded Gertrude Hawley, "that work in the field of physical education is all sport and good times. There is another side to the story. It is true that there are openings in physical education for the girl who is strong, who enjoys sports and games and gymnasium work and who can take the necessary training. But it is also true that it is often very strenuous work. In the school where she teaches, too much may be expected of the young woman in charge of the gymnasium. Her schedule may be crowded to the limit and even the strongest, under such circumstances, becomes fatigued. The equipment given her with which to carry on her class work may be inadequate—yet the finest of results are expected of her. I could name difficulty after difficulty that will overtake her, at some time or other! When I tell you of what we have been doing in our department at Northwestern University, I would not be giving you an adequate picture of it if I did not admit the difficult days, the discouragements and the mistakes. They have all been there! Nothing is ever as easy as it sounds."

She looked at me steadily with her brown eyes and I had a sense of difficulties squarely faced, courageously met.

"But what of that if you like your work, as I do?" she went on with a smile. "There are difficulties in everything. If you can find something which you enjoy, the compensations will outweigh the discouragements for you. And to me, the real fun that I have among my girls, the feeling which I have that it is truly worthwhile to help develop strong bodies, more than outweighs whatever difficulties I do meet."

From the top of a Fifth Avenue bus I waved goodbye to her, then watched her disappear into the hurrying crowd, her tennis racquet lightly swinging from her hand. Gertrude Hawley— director of physical education.

MARION DURELL

*A girl
who didn't know
she wanted to be
a nurse*

MARION DURELL

IN 1856, through the rough barracks of the Crimea, walked a Lady with a Lamp. There was compassion on her face and compassion in her hands. But the compassion was not a sterile thing; it expressed itself, quietly, in blanketing a soldier who slept, in cooling a fevered forehead, in comforting, in re-dressing a wound. Through her ministrations, this "charnel-house of misery" had been converted into a well-managed hospital. Through her leadership, the death rate of those Crimean soldiers had been reduced from fifty per cent to two percent. The Lady with the Lamp was Florence Nightingale, the founder of trained nursing.

In 1926, a Woman in White took the temperature of a patient who had lain, for many desperate days, in the New York City Hospital on Welfare Island, and prepared to go off duty for the night. All day the sick old woman had said nothing to her nurse. In her wretchedness, she had

submitted to the warm bath, the alcohol rub, the
hypodermics, the brushing of her hair, and the
kind words. But now she looked after the nurse
in consternation.

"You ain't goin'?"

"Yes"—very gently.

"But you's comin' back tomorrow, ain't y'?"

"Yes."

The old woman sank to her pillow.

"Praises be for that!" she murmured, and
resigned herself to the pain.

The Woman in White was Marion Durell.

Florence Nightingale is gloriously dead.
Marion Durell, one of her multitudinous suc-
cessors in the nursing profession, is gloriously
alive. She is, in fact, at the present time director
of nurses in the City Hospital of New York.
Two factors, she tells me, were active in turning
her to this particular form of public service—first,
the great need for trained nurses accentuated, in
1918, by the World War; second, something
Florence Nightingale once said:

"Of all the women I know, nurses are the
happiest."

I asked Marion Durell if from her long experience in nursing she agreed with this world-
famous leader.

"Yes," said Miss Durell decisively. "Nursing
seems to me the most satisfying of all occupa-

tions. It demands the best in a woman. Brain,
heart, body, are pressed into service. I hadn't
been in the profession a month before I knew it
was the only work for me. You see, it was like
this. After my graduation from Wellesley in
1908, I tried doing nothing; and then for five
years I tried teaching mathematics at Lawrence-
ville with my father; and then for five years I
tried raising cranberries with my brother on a
farm in southern New Jersey."

"And you weren't happy?"

"I realize now that I wasn't really happy until
I entered nursing. I went through two and a half
years of training in a hospital; then I was staff
nurse at the Henry Street Settlement for four
months; then I returned to private case nursing
for six months; then I was assistant director
of nurses at City Hospital for three years; now
I am director. And all along the way I've been
happy!"

She didn't have to protest it. The confession
was in her blue eyes and around her generous
mouth. But there was something else too. Her
white uniform, neatly starched, spoke of com-
petency; her white cap, striped with a band of
black velvet and sitting perkily on her corn-silk-
colored hair, had an unmistakable look of precision. She had thrown her blue cape over the
back of the chair. Its gay lining made a yellow
pool all about her.

Commenting upon her late entry into nursing, I asked:

"Don't most girls get an idea they wish to be nurses when they are still in high school?"

"Often earlier than that," said Miss Durell. "A recent questionnaire in New York hospitals showed that the great majority of nurses become interested in nursing while they are still in grammar school."

I remembered a schoolmate of mine who insisted, at the age of ten, on playing "hospital." Every automobile she saw was an "ambulance." Her dolls were constantly ill. The cat was forever being bandaged and put on an unappreciated diet. By the time she was thirteen years old, she had definitely decided to be a nurse. Eventually she was. And is.

Not so Marion Durell. Mathematics and cranberries got between her and the profession of nursing. Yet all her life she had been a nurse by instinct, and hadn't known it. Even when she entered upon her training she did not realize how much to her taste the work would be. But her days of actual nursing soon showed her that at last she had found her place.

"Every day it is a joy," said Miss Durell, "to be with my patients. I wish I had come to this work sooner."

It seems strange that she didn't gravitate to nursing when she was a girl. Because she was

always trying to ease suffering when she saw it.
As a high school girl she was able to dispel the
violent headaches of her mother by massaging
just the right nerve centers and rubbing her
temples with cologne. As a college girl, while
vacationing in New Hampshire, she didn't lose
her equilibrium in the presence of two drowned
people. Two young people were thrown out of
a boat and unable to swim. Marion was sitting
on the porch when the cry came. "Help!"
"Drowning!" The victims were brought in. The
other women on the porch were helpless. Marion
alone remembered the principles of resuscitation
taught her in high school. She it was who drained
the water from the lungs. She it was who admin-
istered a hypodermic although her effort was
hopeless from the start.

"You were ready," I said, "and adequate in
the emergency."

She was modest. She declared that she hadn't
done anything unusual at all, that on this occasion—as today, in the operating room—the
needs of another merely overcame her own
squeamishness. When a life hangs in the balance,
she told me, no nurse can hesitate, absorbed in
her own feelings. She has something important
to do. Much depends upon the steadiness of her
hand, and she must answer the challenge valiantly
if she is to be adequate to the need.

"Have you ever known a nurse to faint in the

operating room?" I am afraid this was plain
curiosity on my part.

"Never," said Miss Durell. There was a rec-
ognizable pride in her voice.

And then she told me, briefly, about training.
The period varies in different hospitals. At the
City Hospital it is two and a half years in length.
In many places it is three years. Every phase
of nursing is both studied and practiced. The
apprentice (for that is what she is) divides her
time between the classroom and the sickroom.
She is taught such subjects as physiology, sanita-
tion, dietetics, and care of infants, in addition
to the care of the sick. To her lot falls much routine work—enough to test even the stoutest
hearted, although such work as scrubbing up is
now done in most hospitals by ward maids, not by
student nurses. Yet if she is firm in her purpose
she endures.

The girl who is interested in nursing should
know that although some schools require as little
as one year of high school for entrance, most hospitals are asking more. Many require a four-
year high school course or even college training
as a preliminary. Directors of nurses recognize
the fact that the more general education a girl
can secure before she starts upon her special
nurse's course, the better equipped she will be
to meet the inevitable crises with which every
nurse is confronted.

Young women with college training plus their trained nurse's certificate are prepared for the more important positions in the nursing world. The Yale School of Nursing requires that all young women who enter for training shall have had twenty-eight months of college work.

When one stops to consider that a human life may depend upon what a nurse does in fifteen minutes, one realizes how important it is that every nurse have thorough knowledge of her profession. It is this which is leading hospitals everywhere to ask more and more preliminary education of the young women who enter there for nurses' training. It is this which is making the training course itself more and more thorough.

It was Florence Nightingale who said, "Nursing requires as hard a preparation as any painter's or sculptor's apprenticeship; for what is having to do with dead canvas and cold marble compared with having to do with the living body? There is no such thing as amateur art; there is no such thing as amateur nursing."

When the hospital training is completed and a young woman has secured her nurse's certificate, she may choose from a variety of possibilities. At most times there are more opportunities for nurses than nurses themselves.

She may remain in the hospital, doing what is called "hospital nursing." Here she may become especially interested in the work of the operating

room or of the surgical wards. She may wish to
work chiefly with babies and their mothers, with
crippled children, or other special cases—a wide
range of work.

If she remains in the hospital and shows that
she has the ability to direct the work of others,
she may in time become a director of nurses,
as Marion Durell has become. Every hospital
has its director of nurses, all of them women
who have reached their present positions because
they have proved themselves to be not only
nurses of skill, but administrators.

If she has genuine teaching ability, she may
become an instructor of student nurses in a hospital nurses' school, and there is a real demand
for them.

If, however, a nurse prefers it, she may undertake private cases or accept a position in connection with a school or other organization. Most
of us have met nurses of private cases who have
assumed charge of the care of one sick person,
at home or in a private room of a hospital or
sanitarium.

And we know that private schools and colleges
employ their own nurses. So, too, do many
hotels, stores and factories. The nurses in them
are on duty at certain hours to care for any
emergencies that may arise as well as assisting
in any general health work, such as physical examinations, which the establishment has under-

taken. Young women who enjoy traveling have
even served as nurses on ocean liners, although
such positions are limited in number.

And there are today increasing opportunities
in what is known as public health nursing. Visiting nurses' associations employ nurses to go into
the homes of those whom they wish to help, not
only to care for those who are actually ill, but to
teach the ways by which each family can be kept
well. More and more, doctors are engaged in
preventing illness, as well as in curing it. The
work of visiting nurses is as often concerned with
proper diet for children, with methods of personal and home cleanliness, as it is in caring for
a sick person. This work is that of health education and is offering to nurses today a widening
field.

Visiting nurses are employed by charitable organizations, schools and civic organizations as
well as by some states, counties, cities and towns.
Public clinics not only give needed treatment to
the sick. They carry on health education through
physical examinations and suggestions for the
forming of desirable health habits. Doctors and
nurses work together in these public health
clinics in their work of prevention as well as of
curing.

It is this conception of the work of doctors
and nurses which has brought to both new opportunities. A trained nurse need no longer remain

in a hospital or with private cases. Public health nursing is constantly opening new doors to her.

"There are several things about nursing that I especially like," said Miss Durell as she leaned across her desk toward me. "One is that hospital experience is what I call a negotiable security. There are few places where a nurse cannot find an opening, which means that she can travel and work where she wishes, if she feels so inclined. And she can change from one branch of nursing to another, if she desires."

"But the difficulties of nursing?" I asked. "What are they?"

"The difficulties? They exist, as well as the advantages."

And Marion Durell urges every girl who is attracted to nursing to face them honestly. Nursing drains the strength. Only the girl who has splendid health should attempt it. There is constant need for patience. A nurse must quietly adapt herself to many kinds of dispositions, often those made irritable by illness. There is much to be done that is far from romantic. The hours are long. Very few hospitals have adopted the eight-hour day, and practically none of them has less than a twelve-hour night.

There is, however, a national organization of nurses which is working to better these conditions. This organization is endeavoring to shorten the too-long hours, to give more adequate pay, to create more comfortable living conditions for nurses on hospital staffs, as well as to establish the highest standards for the work itself.

And contrary to the general conception, Miss Durell says that contact with suffering and death does not overwhelm nurses. If one patient dies in a ward there are thirty patients who counteract the gloomy effect of the nearby death by thriving on their treatment. Even death is not always depressing. Miss Durell assured me that a nurse learns to see it philosophically, especially if the patient is old. Sympathy and detachment— she must preserve an even balance between the two. The constant sight of suffering, then, may in Miss Durell's opinion be stricken off the list of disadvantages.

But the advantages. They, too, are to be considered. As Miss Durell said, the training requires no large financial outlay since, usually, the student's services cover her tuition in the hospital as well as her living expenses. Salaries begin early. Immediately upon graduation the nurse may begin her work, since every hospital has need for nurses. There is no expensive outfit to keep up and, as long as her health is good, she has an assured income. Nor need she remain prosaically in one vicinity, unless she wishes.

I looked at Marion Durell, a woman giving herself unstintingly to the profession which she has chosen—and I glanced from the window at the quiet waters which surround Welfare Island. White-breasted gulls were clinging far out to a rock. A little boat went tranquilly down to the bay. Who could believe that this gray quietude hemmed in the suffering? It was a place for gulls, nothing but gulls! Suddenly the white-breasted birds rose in a great company.

"Tell me," I said, "what is the happiest thing in your work?"

"The happiest thing," said Marion Durell, "is this. A poor broken piece of humanity singles you out from the other nurses in the ward and boasts to the next cot, very proudly, *'That's my nurse.'*"

ANNE CARROLL MOORE

A girl
who loved
books and children

ANNE CARROLL
MOORE

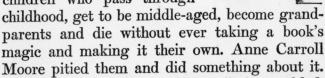

CHILDREN read books and leave little smudge-marks on the fly leaves and are enchanted. Pity, then, the children who pass through childhood, get to be middle-aged, become grand-parents and die without ever taking a book's magic and making it their own. Anne Carroll Moore pitied them and did something about it.

"I have always loved children," she confided, "and books. I'm very lucky to combine the two."

Very lucky. Anne Carroll Moore is head of the children's department in the Public Library of New York City. The marble corridors are her front yard; the library lions which guard the Fifth Avenue entrance know her as well as they know the pigeons that come looking for adventure—or is it crumbs? Long before the present library was built, Anne Carroll Moore "lived" there, in imagination and in the dreams which she helped to make come true. Faithfully and

light-heartedly, she has persevered in the work
which, back in 1896, she chose as her life profession.

The children's room in a public library! Four-
year-olds and five-year-olds, all the way up to
fifteen and sixteen-year-olds. Boys. Girls. Books.
Picture books and story books and things-
to-make books. And every five-year-old, every
nine-year-old, every fifteen-year-old wanting a
book that's just right, not too young, not too
old—just right. Sometimes wishing to discover
that book for themselves, other times wishing to
draw on the knowledge and experience of the
librarian.

There is a special corner for the more grown-up
boys and the taller girls, of course. There they
may go without being called "children." There
they find books gathered together especially for
them by their friend, the understanding librarian.

And, always, there is that other corner. The
one where the chairs are low and the tables are
low and the shelves are low. To step into this
corner is like stepping into Lilliput. The only
thing disproportionately big is the librarian who
moves about, putting back a book, stamping a
card with red ink, collecting a penny for a late
return, buttoning up a small overcoat. Books of
adventure, fairy tales, nonsense stories, wood-
craft instructions, sea yarns line the walls. What
would the world be without children's books?

Anne Carroll Moore has always maintained, inside her, the heart of a child. The heart of a child. . . . Is there anything more lovely? There are willows, of course, and red haws, and streams that go in and out, in and out. But compared to children, these lack glamour. For willows are willows, and red haws are red haws, but every child is different from every other child, being full of wonder and—whether from America, or Chili, or the Gobi Desert—unstandardized.

"Children have distinct and different personalities," Miss Moore told me. "Socially they seem to me much more interesting than most grown people."

She is a brown-burr of a woman, although much slimmer than any brown-burr discovered under a tree. Years ago, as the youngest in the Moore family, she must have been a little witch.

That was in Maine.

She had a triple education: the companionship of her father as they jogged over New England roads; an old village academy; and Bradford Academy in Massachusetts. Then, as she herself delightfully puts it, she "inherited some children." They were nieces—one four years old, one seven years old—and she had long hours in which to play games with them, and read books with them, and grow wise with them.

"We set up," said Miss Moore, "a very intimate relationship."

Later she went to Pratt Institute in Brooklyn to study the science of library work. Is it strange that, loving children and loving books, she gravitated to the headship of the children's room which Pratt opened that very year? It was a new project. Up to that time, the reading public between the ages of four and fourteen had never been taken very seriously. But those deeply interested in children were soon to change this, Anne Carroll Moore among them.

She spent ten years in the children's room of the Pratt Institute Free Library, working to discover just the kind of library children would like best. She watched to see which books naturally interested them, which stories, told aloud, most absorbingly held their attention. She placed books where small hands could reach them. And she invited to the children's room grown-up friends of children to help her in her work. For it was never her plan to work alone. Wherever she found someone who could bring delight to the children, that person was brought to share in the new project—those who could tell stories, those who could arrange fascinating little exhibits, those who could make dashing posters, those who could do any one of a number of other things. The children's room of the Pratt Library quickly became a center not only for children but for those who loved them and wished better to understand them.

"It was great fun to have nothing to go by," said Miss Moore when I saw her in her office. "The Pratt Library was eager for us to try any plan which seemed good—and we did. Today there is a great deal of literature about children's rooms. In those days, we had only our own experiences and those of others who were experimenting in other places. But we did our best to share it all through letters and visits."

The children of Brooklyn responded to Anne Carroll Moore's love of them, to her love of books and her understanding of which books they would most enjoy. They responded to the friendliness they never failed to find in those whom they met in the children's room. They were not preached to about this book or that. When they declared they didn't like a book, they were not told that "every boy and girl ought to like it. It is one of the great books of the world." Their opinions were respected. Their right to personal likes and dislikes was respected. And every effort was made that there might be in that children's room books of all kinds, for all kinds of boys and girls.

They came to regard the room as *theirs*. And Miss Moore and her associates had their important part in the great work of convincing grown-ups that the reading public between the ages of four and fourteen is an important public, worthy of every thoughtful consideration.

When she became head of the children's department of the New York Public Library, she undertook the task of planning libraries for all the children of Manhattan, the Bronx and Staten Island. But Anne Carroll Moore did not think of the children's department as a number of library rooms. She thought of it as belonging to children wherever they were in New York. And she knew that she and her assistants must go out to the children as well as bringing the children to the libraries.

To help her in this work, here, too, she gathered about her those who were especially gifted in work with children. Young women who were interested in becoming children's librarians came from many parts of the country to work in the department. Today, in each of the forty-seven branch libraries of New York City, there is a children's room which is part of the children's department. Members of Miss Moore's department go out to the schools, talking with teachers and parents, arranging that desired books be sent to them. Story-tellers go out to the branch libraries, to playgrounds, and to children's club rooms in settlements and schools. The work is wide and varied—even to seeing that children's books are not forgotten on the book wagon which goes about Staten Island taking books to those in remote districts, far from any library building.

So it has come about that the children's room

of the Fifth Avenue Library building is a center not only for children but for those who are interested in children. If you were to happen in during children's book week, you would find yourself in a distinguished gathering of publishers and editors and writers of children's books and magazines, not forgetting fathers and mothers and teachers. Lining the walls of the room you would see new books and old books, including the famous collection of children's books of other centuries. You would hear talk of children and their reading. And before you left, you might be listening to an attractive young woman, a member of Anne Carroll Moore's staff, tell a story. For Anne Carroll Moore never forgets that everyone loves a story. Small children. And grown-up children.

Today, the interest in children's reading extends around the world. Librarians from other countries visit the United States to see what our children's rooms are like, always bringing us, Miss Moore says, new ideas for our own libraries. Letters from all parts of the world crowd her mail. And books from all parts of the world have been sent to her until her office has become a colorful corner, a place to browse with delight.

For twenty years Anne Carroll Moore has held her present position in the New York Public Library. She isn't nineteen any more. But I'll wager that at nineteen she was less exuberant than she is

today. She has never agreed to stop growing or
exploring. She has never narrowed her vision by
reading only children's books, or only books for
older people. That is why her reviews of children's
books, which appear in *The Bookman,* are
authoritative. That is why "The Three Owls,"
her weekly page in *Books* of the New York Her-
ald-Tribune is as wise as—three owls. That is
why her own books, *Roads to Childhood* and
Crossroads to Childhood, make the books she
mentions real to you, if you have never read them,
or bring back vividly to you your own favorites.
No better list of books has been assembled for
girls than the one in *Crossroads to Childhood*
called "In the Teens."

"A children's room," says Anne Carroll
Moore, "should express the best traditions of a
home, for it *is* a home for all children. The surroundings should be attractive and artistic. The
librarian should look upon herself as hostess, the
children as her distinguished guests. If a little
Russian wanders in, he shouldn't be made to feel
like a stranger in a strange land. Nor a little
Italian. Nor a little French child."

When she speaks of French children, Miss
Moore wears a very special glow. After her trip
to France in 1921, she wrote, "Children are as
vital to the landscape of France as the birds, the
trees, the flowers of the gardens and spring
forests, the light of her sky."

"What girls do you think should become children's librarians?" I asked her.

Anne Carroll Moore smiled in her brown-burr fashion. And I knew that there among books and children she has discovered a richness and variety of experience which some women miss.

"What girls?" she repeated. "Those whom children love spontaneously. Those who love children and who love books continuously. Those who know books well enough to satisfy children and to inspire confidence in their fathers and mothers and teachers."

Just then Paul arrived. He had two apple cheeks, knee breeches, and a grin. All boy. Evidently he and Miss Moore were old friends. They shook hands gravely. And stood together, talking. Something about poetry. . . . I remembered a stray remark of Miss Moore's, "If children are given a natural exposure to poetry, they like it."

Paul did. Paul discussed poetry with Miss Moore, frankly, without embarrassment, without a momentary shuffling of the feet. She looked him in the eyes. She grasped his hand. She showed on her face unmistakable pleasure and no condescension. She was sorry when the apple cheeks and the grin backed through the library door.

Do you love books? Does library work attract you? There is opportunity for you to enter it, if you wish. A recent census shows that ninety-two per cent of the librarians of this country are *not men*.

High school graduates may become assistant librarians without further school training, if they will take special training such as is given in connection with many libraries in our large cities. But if you can afford it, enter one of the special schools for librarians which fit you for the more important positions in the library world.

These library schools are to be found in many parts of this country. And if you wish to combine your library training with your college work, it is possible to do that, too. The state universities of California, Wisconsin, Illinois, Michigan and Western Reserve are among those which enable a young woman to do this. So, too, do Carnegie Institute in Pittsburgh, Columbia University in New York City, Simmons College in Boston and Pratt Institute in Brooklyn, Miss Moore's alma mater. Your own librarian will tell you about these library courses and what they teach.

Such library training will prepare you for the special kind of library work which attracts you. You may wish to become a children's librarian as did Anne Carroll Moore. It is an important work and a merry work. But if you do not care for children, you may choose one of various other kinds of library positions. The general circulating room may be to your taste. The reference department of some library will give you an opportunity to be of service to those who wish to secure books and information along special lines. In the hundreds of public libraries which are today established in this country, there are many departments and many kinds of library work.

There are, too, special libraries. Business houses, banks, life insurance companies and newspapers have their own libraries. If you are interested in any one of these fields, you may be able to find an opening there. The library commissions of our state capitals offer still further choice, one of the most interesting being the traveling libraries through which books are packed and sent out to remote parts of the state. There are libraries in high schools and grammar schools where many a librarian is today showing boys and girls that books are not "lessons" alone. Young women with library training are putting it to good use in book shops—some, even, are establishing such shops of their own.

"But the difficulties?" I asked Anne Carroll Moore.

"Difficulties?" she repeated. "Of course there are difficulties. The hours are long. A librarian often has night work. Librarians' salaries are not what they should be, although they are getting better. And there are the difficulties which always seem to exist whenever you set out to do work of any kind—you may not be given enough money to carry out your plans; you may not have sufficient help; those who should support you with their interest may be indifferent.

"But what of that? The work without difficulties doesn't exist. And the true librarian finds her work itself so full of possibilities and compensations that, although she continues to face the difficulties and work to overcome them, nevertheless they are of less significance to her than her opportunity. For the four walls of a library do not limit you. As librarian you can go with your books to the people in any part of the community where you live. And you may go out to other communities to share your experience and to gain fresh inspiration. Through the years, my own work has taken me to Maine and to Iowa, to North Carolina, to Virginia, to Utah and to France.

"Yes, to me library work is full of significance for the girl who loves books—and people."

ETHEL BARRYMORE

A girl who was always
surrounded by the atmosphere
of the stage

ETHEL
BARRYMORE

"COME in!"
It was a deep
voice, a resonant voice,
an unforgettable voice. It had belonged, an hour
earlier, to an imperious *Portia* on the stage of
the Walter Hampden Theater, a *Portia* as flam-
ingly conceived as the picture which hangs in the
Metropolitan. It belonged now to Ethel Barrymore.

I went in.

I had come to interview the great actress in
her dressing room. She was handsomer, in this
red Renaissance bodice, than the press notices
had ever intimated. Through the mascharo and
the paint, her boldly beautiful features stood out,
uncompromising. Now I knew why John Singer
Sargent wanted to paint her; why Henry James
told her when she was in London that she reminded him of a "Gothic cornice on a Gothic
building."

But this admiration of mine wasn't interview-
ing.

I must get down to the questions-and-answers
of the day. Didn't she ever tire of the stage?
Never—although she has been acting since she
was fourteen. Did she consider practical experience behind the footlights or a course in a school
of dramatic art the best training for a beginner?

Experience. Experience, she explained, seemed
to her the legitimate way to learn posture, and
enunciation and pantomime and handplay. One
by one, Miss Barrymore's theories came to light;
one by one, the facts of her adventurous life. She
was most gracious in the telling.

Ethel Barrymore comes from histrionic stock.
Her grandmother was Mrs. John Drew, of *Mrs.
Malaprop* fame, whose actor-husband died
young. Her father was Maurice Barrymore, an
English actor; her mother, Georgie Drew Barrymore; her uncles, John Drew, the younger, and
Sidney Drew; her brothers, John Barrymore
and Lionel Barrymore. Without an exception,
they were actors. Is it strange, then, that Ethel
early turned to the stage? Yet Miss Barrymore,
when confronted by the question, insists that she
originally took to acting, not because she loved
it, but because she had to earn a living.

"The truth is," she said, "I was never particularly interested in child-plays, although I took
part in them, just as all children do. When I
was at the Convent of Notre Dame, I thought
I'd be a musician, probably because at nine I won

a medal for playing Beethoven. My great love for the theater came later."

When Ethel was fourteen, her mother died in California, the mother whom she has since called "the gayest and most gallant person I ever knew." Matured by the sorrow, Ethel, alone and as gallant as the dead, brought the body across the continent to New York. That year she twisted up her hair and wore a black dress. The next year, joining her grandmother in Montreal, she was given her first small part, *Julie,* the maid in *The Rivals*. The winter in Canada was ill-starred. It was followed by many vigils in the outer offices of New York theatrical agencies—many vigils and no success.

For two years she played only small parts with any company that would take her on. Then she went to London with William Gillette in *Secret Service*. London was, to her, the fabulous city. She remained there with Ellen Terry and Sir Henry Irving after the *Secret Service* company had dispersed. When she returned to America, Charles Frohman became her manager and her valued friend. Under his guidance she played *Madame Trentoni,* her first real part, in *Captain Jinks of the Horse Marines,* the play which made her a star, *Cousin Kate, The Country Mouse, Carrots, Sunday, The Doll's House, The Silver Box* by Galsworthy, *Alice-Sit-by-the-Fire, Mid-Channel* by Pinero, *The Twelve Pound Look,* her first vaudeville vehicle, *Tante,* and *Our Mrs. McChesney.* When he went down on the *Lusitania,* Miss Barrymore summed up her whole impression of the great producer by saying, "He had a golden heart."

By this time, Ethel Barrymore, as well as her brilliant brothers, was established in the heart of the theater-going public. The rôles which she has since played have been various, but to them all she has brought a keen intelligence, penetration and appreciation, as well as a willingness to work and to admit her mistakes. These rôles include *The Lady of the Camellias,* Miss Barrymore's favorite, and *Déclassée,* the public's favorite.

"An actor's salvation," says Miss Barrymore, "is the assuming of many parts.

"No, I have never done Lady Macbeth," she adds regretfully. "But I shall!"

It is her genuine love for the theater which has carried her through much hard work, some privations, and the complications of marriage and motherhood. Her three children, Sammie, Sister, and Jackie, were born in short breathing spaces between engagements. She tells gleefully of telephoning Mr. Frohman two hours after the birth of Jackie to announce that she had "an awfully nice baby" and expected to be at rehearsal very soon. Ten days later she was acting in the play called *Tante.* When asked how she can be a mother and an actress at the same time, she invariably replies:

"I was born, and so, I have always understood, was my mother. Neither my mother nor my grandmother forsook the theater because of motherhood. Why should I? It is natural for me to be an actress and it is natural for me to be a mother. If an actress has an average amount of common sense, she can organize her life as a regular human being."

I wanted to ask if her profession had made her a stranger to her children. I hesitated. She anticipated the question.

"And I don't neglect my children, either. Until they went off to school, I saw them as much as most mothers see theirs. When I am compelled to be absent, I write them every day and they write me every day. They are always in reliable hands. Our summers at Mamaroneck have been glorious."

The children, it seems, are too young to know whether they, too, like their illustrious forebears, will learn first-hand the ways of wigs and make-up, cues and curtain-calls, footlights and stage-props, and the palpitations of a "first night." Yet Sammie has already distinguished himself in school plays. Sister says her ambition is to act "like mother." And little Jackie, the youngest, when asked recently if he would grow up to be an actor, made this statement:

"Oh, I don't know. Maybe I might be a comedy."

Ethel Barrymore is mellowed by her memories. She remembers how as a child at her grandmother's house in Philadelphia she was initiated into the drama by stage quotations from *The Tomb of the Capulets*. When she ordered Ethel to bed, this tender and terrifying woman, owner of the Arch Street Theater, would say, "Stand not upon the order of your going, but go at once!" One cannot overestimate the part which this early initiation into stage ways has played in Miss Barrymore's attainments.

Today she remembers how, the first time she played in Philadelphia, the audience shouted, "Ethel, you're all right. We remember your grandmother. We love you!"

Her life has been rich in friends, in England and America—Mark Twain, William Vaughn Moody, Maxfield Parrish, Richard Harding Davis, Anthony Hope, William Allen White, and many more. She remembers "all the shine, all the rain" of a varied and colorful career. And with her Gothic head held high, she vows that there is much to be appended.

For her place is in the theater. She was born in its tradition. She grew up under its influence. Her elations and her discouragements are tightly bound up with it. Ethel Barrymore would not be Ethel Barrymore if she forsook the stage.

But what of the girl who has not had the advantage of early acquaintance with the stage, yet who is interested in it? She may be a girl who, in the cast of her high school play, listens to the admiring applause of her friends, to their exclamations of delight over her performance and their remarks that, "You ought to go on the stage, my dear!"

What must such a girl do if she is serious in her plan? Much. To Ethel Barrymore was given an unusual inheritance. Her home surroundings brought her into intimate association with the stage from her earliest childhood. She grew up hearing about it, absorbing its atmosphere from the members of her family and her friends. To this experience was added the advantage of her unusual personality and appearance. Nevertheless, even Ethel Barrymore's place in our theater has not been achieved without effort.

Real dramatic ability, great determination, great love of dramatic art, physical strength to endure strenuous work—these a girl must have who would win distinction in the profession of acting or even opportunity to enter it.

Taking part in high school plays, college plays, Little Theater plays, in any plays that are at hand will be somewhat of a guide to her, although a less important one than the amateur is prone to believe. But if through them a girl discovers a real taste for the work, it will be necessary for

her to make the same choice which confronts
many girls in other lines of work—that of attending a school and taking training there or of acquiring needed experience in the profession itself.
Those on the professional stage who never attended such a school are apt to discount its advantages, just as those in other fields of work who
never attended special training courses often discount them. Yet today, with the wider recognition of the importance and the possibilities of
the stage, has come a deepening realization of
what excellent courses in this work may mean,
courses in such subjects as voice culture, phon-
etics, English diction, physical training, stage
mechanics, stage business, costuming, make-up
and the study of dramatic literature. These
courses may save a beginner much time and effort
in her struggle.

If a school, then choose one which is recognized
as excellent. In it a girl can test her own ability
and preferences. Certain of our best schools today frankly state that one purpose of their work
is to discover for their students whether or not
they have sufficient ability to warrant continuing
their work upon the stage. *The Theater Guild*
regards this weeding out as second to nothing in
importance.

"A girl must be willing to face the facts about
herself," they say.

But whether a young woman starts directly

upon the professional stage or from special training in a school of dramatic art, she eventually
comes to the long road over which Ethel Barrymore and all other actresses without exception
have traveled—the road of actual stage experience; of assuming many parts to learn flexibility;
of taking parts that are uncongenial in order to
appear at all; of rehearsing in a play only to find
that the public does not like it; of haunting managers' offices in the hope of securing a part and
meeting in those offices often hundreds of other
aspirants for the same rôle (for there are always
more young women eager to go upon the stage
than there are openings for them); of making a
little money go a long way; of never being certain
of employment.

These are the difficulties which the young stage
aspirant is certain to meet, and they are great.
Even those who have attained distinction in the
drama are never certain of an engagement, from
one year to the next. Those who are associated
with the theater have many stories to tell of actors
who have served a long and strenuous apprenticeship in minor rôles, some never to emerge
from them, others to emerge but for a short time.

Nevertheless, to those who feel the appeal of
the theater strongly, these difficulties are not
insuperable. Young women are today winning
their way upon the stage. Some, like Ethel Barrymore, have had years of association with it. Others

are newcomers. All have had varying degrees of education.

But what of the girl who discovers that her love for stage work and her determination to enter it are not matched by her acting ability and who honestly admits the fact to herself? She may still be associated, in other capacities, with this field which so attracts her. It is possible that she may discover in herself the characteristics of leadership, the quick appreciation and appraisement of the details of production and the discriminating taste which will qualify her for work in the production of plays. Women are becoming producers of plays in the professional theater as well as in the Little Theater playhouses throughout the country.

Ability to direct the production of plays is also in demand in college and normal schools, high schools and boarding schools. Here the work is combined with teaching, in most instances, but a young woman nevertheless has opportunity to employ her producing talent. All the experience which a young producer is able to secure through actual contact with the professional stage is of use to her. Experience in pantomime, in voice placement, in lighting, in planning stage sets, in make-up—no detail is too small to be unimportant to the general effect of a play. One young woman whose work includes the directing of plays as well as teaching in the English department in a girls' school recently spent her vacation in acting minor parts with a stock company, returning to her directing with an intimate knowledge of the actual requirements and methods of professional stage work.

A girl's interest in plays in high school may lead her to specialize in dramatic literature in college and so to the teaching of it when she graduates. Girls of literary ability may turn to the writing of plays, with a period of apprenticeship as inevitable for them as for those who aspire to acting itself. Courses in an increasing number of colleges are offering students not only the opportunity of writing their own plays, but of actually producing them, of designing and executing the costumes, of painting the scenery, even of manipulating the lighting.

Of such things Ethel Barrymore and I talked, that day in her dressing room, until it was time for her to go. As I rose, she began to brush a yellow something which she had gingerly removed from her head. Against the velvet of her Italian gown, it looked more yellow than ever.

She held it up. "A back wig," she explained, in her dark and enthralling voice.

MABEL E. STEWART

A girl who had
no special talent
but had to go to work

MABEL E. STEWART

SHE shivered as she took dictation from the Distinguished Gentleman. For the Distinguished Gentleman was Chairman of the Board of Directors, Irving Bank and Trust Company; and she was only a small person with a big ambition. She shivered so hard that the dashes in her shorthand turned out to be wiggles. But the Distinguished Gentleman was never allowed to see her fright; never allowed to see that a little scared rabbit, not a private secretary at all, was manufacturing dots and scratches on a thick pad of paper.

That was six years ago. Now Mabel Stewart has a poise which befits her position as secretary to the chairman of the board. When she takes dictation, her hand is firm. When she answers the telephone, she speaks with quiet authority. More than the typewriting which she studied in high school, more than the shorthand, more than the commercial law, six years of actual experience in an office have polished her into a first-class secretary. The magic of six years! And yet the career of private secretary to the head of a great bank requires more than magic. And it requires more than ambition. And more than a neat little figure in a black satin dress, tailored. It requires what Mabel Stewart has in a delightful degree: the manners of a mouse and the heart of a lion.

"There's really nothing to tell about what I did," announced Mabel Stewart just as every nice person announces before the telling of a special story. "It was luck."

Luck! The private secretary to a big official is never a private secretary on luck. Perhaps, in the beginning, luck is a factor but later on something with more iron in it is demanded. *Getting* a job and *keeping* it are not the same. Are you quick? Are you accurate? Are you tactful? Are you gracious? Are you sensible? Have you a good memory for names and faces and facts? These questions, and a hundred more, a business man asks about his secretary, if not in actual words, at least in his harassed mind. The answer, as revealed by her actions from nine o'clock in the morning to five o'clock in the afternoon, decides whether she be praised or peremptorily dismissed.

"Well, at least *partly* luck," amended Miss

Stewart. "In high school I planned to teach. Not that I had any special talent for teaching. Not that I even wanted to teach. But getting to be a teacher seemed to be the best solution—and the easiest—to the problem of earning a few nickels. My mother and father were dead, so the nickels were rather necessary. I had studied shorthand and typing only because they gave me 'points' for graduating and required no home-study! I am being honest, you see. And I had taken commercial law for the same superficial reason—points. Wasn't that luck? I never dreamed that some day I'd want them desperately."

I tried to imagine Mabel Stewart presiding over a roomful of rambunctious youngsters. I couldn't. Here she was in an office, here she belonged.

"But when it came right down to stepping out into teaching, as some of my friends were doing, I didn't want to. I decided that stenographic work in an office appealed to me more and besides I was already trained for it. So I took a position with a corrective eating concern. You'd be surprised how much, on a small scale, I learned in that funny little office. But the corrective eating concern failed. And that was luck for me again—I see it clearly now. Otherwise, I might at this very moment, be writing letters to sell books on when and how and what to eat!"

Curious, the ways of fortune. Sometimes they seem to take you by the nose and lead you, forcibly, in the direction they want you to go.

"And then——" said I, eagerly.

"And then, some way, I thought of banks. The atmosphere of banks appealed to me. I thought I should enjoy working in one. So one bright after· noon I made a pilgrimage down Broadway. Clearly, if I wished to work in a bank, the thing to do was to apply at them. I stopped at eight different banks, inquired for work and filled out application cards. The first place where I stopped, oddly, was the American Exchange Irving Trust Company. It was in September, and a few days later I was notified to report for duty on the first of October. Imagine my jubilation!"

"Jubilation—of course," said I.

"And my fear," added Miss Stewart quickly. "I was in terror, those first few months, lest I move too slowly or mis-spell an important word or show the wrong person out the door. I was in the offices of the chairman of the board of directors, but I started with sub-secretarial work. I did all the filing, all the keeping of routine records, all the uninteresting stenographic work which the head secretary, the private secretary to our chief, scorned. I was more or less of a worm! But a few months later my opportunity unexpectedly arrived. The private secretary, a man, was taken ill and forced to leave the city. He did not return. Our chief decided to try me out, so I shivered at the prospect of this increased responsibility and shook myself into the secretary's place."

Was it possible that this calm little person *ever shivered?*

"Of course I did. Goodness—the chairman of the board of directors! But looking back on how much I didn't know those days, I am sure he must have had a few trepidations himself!"

Mabel Stewart twinkled.

"Anyway, I learned in the harness. That is one advantage of secretarial work. Given your stenography and typing, you can and must get the rest right in your job. For every secretarial position is different, depending upon what your employer does and upon his temperament. The secretary to a publisher, the secretary to a college president, the secretary to a department store head—every one has special duties which go with her particular position. I learned my job in the only way I could learn it by doing, conscientiously, what I was told to do. And by keeping my eyes open. As soon as I saw that any way of doing a certain piece of work disturbed my chief, I did it another way, and another until I discovered the way in which things went most smoothly. Then I continued with that. I wanted to hold my job. To do so, I had to please him. So I studied his ways."

"But these different secretarial jobs," I interrupted. "They have something in common, haven't they?"

"Oh, yes. All secretaries open their employer's mail and arrange it for his inspection, in order of importance; answer the telephone; keep a record of every engagement, and remind their employer when an engagement is imminent; receive and dismiss callers of every color, sex and caste; take dictation and transcribe it; file correspondence; keep check-books so that a bank-balance can be rendered at five minutes' notice; make it a point to be in the office when their employer is out; "tidy" his desk, and lock his desk at the end of a day. And every secretary that ever was, must regard as absolutely confidential the matters which pass through her hands."

Miss Stewart was out of breath from talking, and I was out of breath from listening. So much detail!

"Detail and more detail. That's what secretarial work *means*. But to me it is never monotonous. No two days are alike. The routine is always being broken. New people come to the office, prominent business men, charity solicitors, newspaper reporters, politicians, and riff-raff. It is part of my job to size them up and decide whether

or not their business is worth the time of my
employer. If it isn't I say 'Begone!' or diplomatic
words to that effect. It isn't easy to make them tell
their business. Some of them close up like clams
when they see me. But that's where tact comes
in——"

"And personality," I added under my breath.

She would not concede the personality. But
her brown eyes conceded something else.

"I get more than I give. Why, it's a most
liberal education. I often think business affords
a woman as much training as travel. It certainly
shows you the back-side and the front-side and
the rough selvage of human nature. And in an
office such as this, one picks up a wide knowledge
of present-day affairs, quite different from that
which can be learned from books."

"Are you going to enter banking, itself?" I
asked.

Mabel Stewart shook her head. "No. I have
found what I like to do and I am going to keep
on doing it. But if I were attracted to banking,
I would go into it. Banking has been a field not
usually entered by women. But every year their
number increases. So if you wish to do that kind
of work—why not?"

Why not, indeed!

"Yes," continued Mabel Stewart, "if a girl
is interested in any special field, and if she has
no money to take training in it, I can think of

no better way to serve her apprenticeship than to study stenography and typing and start as secretary to someone who is doing work in that field. You would think, with all the girls who are stenographers, that such an opening would be difficult to find. It really isn't—for no matter how many stenographers there are, there are always more poor ones than excellent ones. And it is the excellent ones for whom employers are looking."

Just then one of the three telephones on Miss Stewart's desk jangled. Mabel Stewart said, "Hello," in a voice cool and efficient.

"I have learned to discriminate," she said, as she hung up the receiver, "between important calls and non-important calls. My chief is an extremely busy man. His time is enormously valuable. I interrupt him only when the call is very urgent. Otherwise, I hear that most dreadful of sentences: 'Miss Stewart, this shouldn't happen again.' Luckily, I can ward off a great number of incoming calls by making appointments if appointments are to be made, writing down brief messages that are sent over the telephone—in fact, wherever I can, I save his time."

"What *can't* you do?" I exclaimed.

Again she twinkled. "Much!" she sighed.

"And when your employer is out of town?"

"I work just the same. Naturally, a little more devolves upon me when he is away, for that is the time when I have to exercise most careful judgment. The office goes right on. Mail comes in regularly, callers come in just the same, and the telephones are seldom quiet. Of course, needless to say, employers, when they go away whether on business or vacation, dislike being bothered too much with office matters. On the other hand, they like to feel that things are receiving proper attention during their absence. I always keep my chief's itinerary on hand, for there are times when it is necessary for me to send telegrams on matters of importance. And the return telegram usually contains instructions that have to be acted upon. There are few idle minutes in this busy office."

So much to do, and yet so bright-eyed! No doubt the duties which seemed so intricate to me had become through long familiarity, simple to her. She plucked a piece of lint from her trim black satin dress.

"I don't lament these odd jobs," she continued. "After all, my work becomes less mechanical each year. I no longer do the filing, or the typing, or the bulk of the dictation. They fall to the stenographer in the outer office, who sits where I did when I began six years ago."

Evidently Mabel Stewart has found, through a little luck and a great deal of pluck, the work which best suits her particular self. As a girl in high school, she liked responsibility, and she liked

precision, and she liked to figure out thus-and-
so about the people she met. Today she combines
all these girl likings in her woman's job.

"But the disadvantages?" I said. "There must
be disadvantages."

Mabel Stewart made three wrinkles between
her eyebrows. "For me? Or for girls in general
who are secretaries?"

"Both."

"Well, I would say the disadvantage of irreg-
ular hours. I am here every morning at eight-
forty-five to get the office in complete readiness
for my chief. But that does not mean I may not
have to stay until seven or eight to get some important work out. Every big executive has times
of unusually strenuous work and that means
equally strenuous days and often evenings for his
secretary. I know a woman whom many girls
envy. She is secretary to one of the best known
Americans. What those girls do not know is how
completely her time is at the call of that man.
Often, she is summoned to his house on Sundays
to do an emergency job for him.

"I am fortunate. While I work late sometimes,
at other times I get off early. I understand the
man I work for and he—after six years— understands me. If he were an ogre, now, I would have
a different story to tell."

She would. I know an employer who is an ogre,

another who is a green dragon, and still another
who is a wild-cat and a donkey all in one.

"Many girls find themselves in uncongenial
surroundings," she concluded. "In such a situation, I think a girl can do one of two things—
save up enough money so that she may resign
and take enough time to find what she wants.
Or perfect herself in her work so that she may
find another position at once. Or both at the same
time! A secretary will never be happy unless she
and her employer understand each other and
work harmoniously together. How could I be
confidential assistant to a man who refused to
have confidence in me? How could I? One or
the other of us, probably both, would come to
grief."

Great grief, I admitted. While the private secretary was fearing her employer, or hating him,
she would surely forget that her job was to save
his time in every way possible, anticipating his
wants, vanishing like a marionette, when need be,
only to reappear like a marionette, upon request.

Great grief, indeed.

INEZ HAYNES IRWIN

*A girl
who always liked
to write*

INEZ HAYNES IRWIN

"WHEN I was seven, I wrote a poem," said Inez Haynes Irwin. "At least, I wrote something that rhymed and the grown-ups around me called it a poem."

We were sitting in the long, softly-lighted living room of her New York home. All about us was the welcoming atmosphere of friendliness. I felt it in the flickering logs of the fireplace, in the old chairs and davenports and tables that seemed to have settled comfortably down, each in its own place. But most of all I felt it in Mrs. Irwin herself.

Years before I had read her *Phoebe and Ernest* stories and had delighted in them. Phoebe and

Ernest were such real folks. I considered them my
friends at once and ever since have regarded them
as such. Now, sitting beside Mrs. Irwin on a
deep-sinking blue davenport, I felt myself responding to her in the same way. And smiling
over her reminiscences just as I had smiled with
Phoebe and Ernest.

As she spoke of her first poem, Mrs. Irwin
laughed merrily. But underneath was the high
seriousness of a woman who can honestly say that
she doesn't remember a time when she didn't
want to write.

"My mother was dumbfounded when I brought
that poem to her. It ran something like this:

> "The sky is blue,
> "And I am true.
>
> "The sun is bright,
> "It is all right."

"And that," said Inez Haynes Irwin, "was my
start.

"I was late in beginning my literary career,"
she continued. "I liked to write. I was constantly
scribbling in my journal or at some idea. But
it did not occur to me to become a professional
writer until some time after college. I think this
was due to the fact that, although I was brought
up in a book-loving family, none of them was a
creative writer. Contrasted with this, my niece,

Phyllis Duganne, grew up in a house where at least two people were at their writing every day, Will Irwin, my husband, and myself, with Wallace Irwin and other writers as frequent visitors. It is not surprising that while she was still in her teens, she started on her own literary career.

"But there was not a time when I did not love writing. I remember how disturbed the other girls were when I announced to our high school teacher that I wished more frequent compositions would be required. At Radcliffe, my favorite course was the one in which we wrote a daily theme. After college, I wrote a twenty-thousand word novelette and a sixty-thousand word novel before anything of mine was published.

"Just as I was finishing the novel, Gelett Burgess came to Scituate where I was living. And to him I owe that debt of gratitude which many a young writer owes to some older friend who from a wider experience gives him wise suggestions about his own work and his future. Mr. Burgess heard that I had written a novel and asked if he might read it. Only too gladly, I gave it to him. He was most kind about it. Today I wonder what he could have seen in it. But looking back I realize that although none of its crudities and inaccuracies escaped comment, he did it with so many excellent suggestions for the novel's improvement that I was filled with hope and confidence.

" 'Why don't you write short stories?' he asked me at the end of an afternoon during which we had discussed my novel and many other things. 'You have told me a dozen short stories, right here, only you have not recognized them. Try writing one, now. And—by the way—if I were you, I would learn to use a typewriter!'

"Because I so greatly admired him, I at once carried out his suggestions. Simultaneously, I started upon a short story and the typewriter! The short story grew to be fifteen thousand words long and I at once took it to Mr. Burgess. He read it, then summoned me for the verdict.

" 'You have an interesting story here—somewhere!' he told me. 'Yes, I think that after you have taken out two or three dozen descriptions of the heroine's hair, you may be able to sell it to a magazine.'

"I knew what he meant—that I had just begun my work on that story, that I must revise and re-write it until it took form as a smooth-running narrative. I did revise and re-write it, many times, just as I still revise and re-write all my stories today. And when I at last returned it to him, he took it to New York and marketed it for me. From that time on I felt myself definitely committed to a writer's career. I knew that I had as yet no self-criticism of my work, and that I did not know how to produce a finished piece of writing. But I resolved to learn. My journal

was filled with studies of life. Yet they were not
stories. For just as tubes of paint are a painter's
medium only, so studies of life are far from being
stories.

"My writing became focused. I concentrated
on short stories, thinking short stories, dreaming
short stories, writing short stories. Ideas bubbled.
It seemed to me I could not work fast enough
to get them down on paper. One week, I remember I wrote six short stories in succession. They
were merely first rough drafts. It was later necessary for me to spend a good deal of time on each
one in order to whip it into final shape. But the
story germs were there.

"At this time, I was not financially dependent
upon the money which I received for my stories.
I was free to experiment as much as I wished.
Nevertheless, having committed myself to the
work of a writer, having assured myself that
despite all possible failures I would keep on until
I was forty, I was not satisfied unless what I wrote
met with acceptance in some magazine. When
the time did come that the income from my
writing was necessary, I had gone through my
writer-apprenticeship.

"As I worked on my short stories, another
dream soon came to me, the dream of doing a
novel. But a novel takes time to write. A writer
must have a sufficient amount of money on which
to live while he is devoting himself to it. As

rapidly as I could, I put aside money for this purpose and as soon as the savings were sufficiently large, I wrote my novel, which was eventually published. From that time to this, my work has consisted of writing short stories, and novels, as well."

To her writing, Inez Haynes Irwin brings the experiences of a varied life. She was born on the Tropic of Capricorn, in the crater of an extinct volcano. Since her parents, who were Americans, lingered only seven months in the vicinity of Rio de Janiero, Brazil, Mrs. Irwin says she will never write the reminiscences of her return. Boston was her next stopping place. She stayed there so long, in the process of growing up and going to school, that she began to wonder whether her life would not be lived in one state. The three years preceding her work at Radcliffe she taught school in the winter and told stories to children during the summer.

Then came her short stories and first novels and years which put an end to her fear lest her life be lived within restricted borders. For she has traveled widely. Accompanying her husband, Will Irwin, on his important newspaper assignments, she has visited every country of Europe, in addition to crossing our own continent many times. She has lived in San Francisco and Paris and New York and has enjoyed her stay in each. For wherever Inez Haynes Irwin goes, she enters

with zest into the life around her, never failing
to find yet further material for her own writing.

She is now dividing her year between Scituate
summers and New York winters. The Irwin
house on Eleventh Street is a buzz of literary
activity. The husband writes; the wife writes; the
niece writes. A honeycomb in the swarming
season is no busier.

"If a girl were to ask you how to start out on
a literary career today," I asked, "what would
you tell her? Would you advise her to go to
college and take courses in how to write, or
what?"

Mrs. Irwin shook her head. "I don't know,"
she replied. "Actually I don't know. For there
isn't any rule which can be applied to everyone.
I would want to know a great deal about the
girl herself before I could answer. I went to college and am glad that I did. That course in daily
theme writing is still helping me. On the other
hand, my niece, Phyllis Duganne, did not attend
college. Before she was twenty, Phyllis had published her first novel. Nothing could keep her
from writing. And she is not sorry she spent
chiefly in writing the years when she might have
been in college instead.

"Do you see? Everything depends upon the
girl herself, what she is like, where she lives, what
she can afford to do. Every girl who writes must
study her own situation.

"I can, however, tell you how some of my young friends are working it out for themselves. What other young women are doing is always suggestive in one way or another. The girl of whom I am now thinking went to college. She loved to write, had been editor of her high school paper, and so gravitated to the English courses in college, taking every writing course offered and being especially grateful, so she now says, for the course in description which gave her a new sense of the delicate distinctions in words. While in college, she earned a considerable amount of money as a member of the press board, sending college news out to the newspapers.

"When she was graduated, it was natural for her to turn to work in which her writing would be of use to her. She had registered with the vocational bureau of the college and through them obtained an opening with the advertising department of a publishing house. Her special work was to assist in the preparing of the catalog of books which is periodically issued by the concern and in writing the brief descriptions of the books (often called 'blurbs') which appear on the paper jackets.

"She is still with this publishing house. She enjoys her work and the atmosphere of books about her. She enjoys the people whom she meets. But she now has another plan. For some time, in the hours outside her office, she has been writing short stories. Some have been accepted. More have not. But she has received enough encouragement to make her wish to experiment still more in her short story writing and she is saving her money so that she may take a year's leave of absence from her position, during which she plans to write.

"I shall be interested in seeing what happens then. Perhaps she will be able to support herself by her 'free lance' writing. A free lance writer is one who has no salaried position but who gives her entire time to her own writing, marketing it with the magazines and newspapers when she can and so trying to support herself. I have known young women who have dreamed of becoming novelists, biographers, short story writers or playwrights who have saved their money just as my friend is doing and who have then stepped out into their free lance work.

"Some have been able to support themselves. Others have not, returning to their paid positions. Rent and board bills are prompt. Checks from magazines are sometimes slow in coming. Every young woman who wishes to experiment continuously in her own creative writing has the problem of support to solve—unless, of course, money is available for her. But such instances are rare.

"Another young friend of mine is a high school graduate. She, too, has writing ability. As soon as she was through high school, it was necessary for her to earn her own living. So she went to work on a newspaper. She worked as sub-assistant on the woman's page, going out to secure items of interest and special stories about prominent women. In time she, too, decided to try her hand at her own writing. But because she then had her mother to support as well as herself, she was forced to write her stories during such few free moments as she had during the day or night.

"She did sell a limited number of her stories and is still doing so. But the market for the kind of stories which she does is restricted. So, to supplement the income from her writing, she is handling the publicity work of a charitable organization. This publicity work consists of keeping in touch with the activities of the organization, gathering items of general interest and seeing that they are released to the newspapers. In the time which remains to her (for the publicity work does not occupy her entire day) she is continuing with her writing of stories.

"I think these two girls are typical of many who like to write and who have writing ability. Their ability makes possible for them positions in advertising agencies or in the advertising departments of commercial concerns of all kinds; they enter newspapers, publishing houses, magazine work or trade journals—anywhere where there is demand for what they can do. Some ultimately decide to leave their positions and enter the field of free lance writing. Others prefer to continue in their newspapers, advertising, magazine or publishing house work.

"On newspapers, the positions today open to women are no longer so limited as formerly. Women are not only engaged in writing fashions or society notes or cooking articles. They are working side by side with men in reporting and even in the executive positions. On one of the leading newspapers of New Jersey, a woman is city editor, a position many have often declared could not be successfully held by a woman. On the staffs of magazines, women are finding congenial work. The apprentice positions usually consist of assisting the editor of some department with the many details of magazine management; of proof reading or of manuscript reading. If a girl decides to remain with a magazine, she may in time be placed in charge of one of the departments, or oven attain an editorship.

"I think most of our editors became editors in some such way as this. They liked to write. They associated themselves with a magazine because of its congeniality and discovered that editorial work appealed to them as a career. I once looked in *Who's Who* for all the editors with whom I am personally acquainted. You would be surprised to know the number who have written a book or two. Pick up the magazines today and you will often find a story or an article by an editor. They still enjoy writing, you see.

"Perhaps that is what makes most of them understanding and sympathetic. I have rarely found editors critical without being constructively so. And I know that they are always on the watch for young writers who give evidence of real talent.

"But to return to the openings for beginners. I wouldn't have you think that they are to be found on every hand. In most of the fields which I have mentioned, available positions are limited in number. Newspaper and magazine opportunities are sometimes lacking, as are those in publishing houses, advertising agencies or trade papers. But they do exist. They can be found in time and with persistence.

"Once having gained her start, every girl must determine her own plan of future action. Shall she continue in a salaried position? Shall she save money for experimenting in writing? Shall she try to find one of the rare part-time paid positions which will enable her to do her own writing part of the time? Shall she continue with her writing if she marries, as so many women writers are doing? These are but few of the questions which will present themselves for an answer.

"But to every girl who likes to write I would say, above all things, keep on writing and writing and writing—anything you wish—and living and living and living. And reading and reading and reading. Form the habit of writing every day. Keep at what you start, even though the first enthusiasm for your idea cools. This is apt to be the experience of every writer before he has completed a piece of work. Develop persistence."

"Suppose you were starting out today, what would you do, Mrs. Irwin?" I asked. "Just what you did?"

"By no means! Whichever road you take, you wish sooner or later that you had taken another. Today, I think I would enter a school of journalism, preparatory to doing work on a newspaper. I should like the friendly rivalry and stimulus of the classroom work. I should like the varied assignments. The professor works out many contrasting experiments in newspaper writing. As a novice on a newspaper, you might not for a long time have opportunity for so wide a variety of journalistic writing. Yes, I should like to attend a school of journalism, I think.

"And then I would go onto a newspaper. I wish I had been a reporter, running around the city on assignments, seeing life as it is lived in every nook and cranny, meeting people such as I have never known, will never know, rushing back to get it all written ahead of the 'dead line,' that last moment before the presses start on the next edition.

"To me, that is experience which I wish I had had. On the other hand, only the other day a friend of mine was bemoaning the fact that her newspaper writing is proving a handicap to her in her writing of short stories. She has now resigned from her newspaper work and is giving her entire time to fiction. She feels that during her years as a newspaper writer, she formed certain habits of style which she must now break.

"And there you are! There isn't any rule. The only answer is that if you like to write, you must write and write and write. And if your ambition is definite enough," Mrs. Irwin concluded—and after twenty-five years of writing, she is qualified to speak—"you will find that everything is grist to the literary mill. If you must take some position far removed from writing, while you are scribbling in your notebooks and upon your stories after hours, you may surely know that every bit of life which is humming around you is providing future backgrounds and atmospheres and incidents and characters for you. Above all, if you believe in yourself and if as you go on you have reason for continued faith in your ability, persist. It is a struggle. And yet——"

"And yet?"

"It is worth while," said Mrs. Irwin, earnestly.

MINNA HALL CAROTHERS

A girl who only gradually
discovered what she
most wished to do

MINNA HALL CAROTHERS

"AT SIXTEEN, I put my two pigtails on top of my head, lengthened my skirts, and joined the teaching staff of my business school, instructing night classes and day classes in the mysteries of Sir Isaac Pitman's stenographic hieroglyphics. Most of my pupils were older than I."

Minna Hall Carothers was telling me, because I had just asked her, about her work. I had come to her because she is one of the best known advertising women in this country. Because she has been president of the New York League of Advertising Women, and is now president of the Federation of Advertising Women's Clubs of the World. But most of all, because I knew she could tell me of opportunities for girls in advertising.

I had opened the door of her office hesitantly, thinking of her achievements. The first minute of our conversation I thought, "Why, this brown little person is a home body." The next minute I thought, "Maybe she was born a home body, but somehow she has evolved in another direction." The third minute I thought, "She is right where she should be—born and bred in the briar patch!"

The briar patch, she explained, was New York City. Like her mother and her grandmother, she is a New Yorker. Her father was an Englishman. The education which she managed to extract from the metropolis was short and to the point—over, as far as going to school was concerned, when she put up her hair and started teaching at the Merchants' and Bankers' Business School.

"It was the only thing to do, you see. We needed more money in the family. I was old enough to earn money. So I did."

Minna Hall Carothers smiled through the definite brown of her eyes, thinking, I knew, of those days when at sixteen she confidently stepped up in front of her classes. But even then those steady brown eyes were looking beyond the business school. For "Peggy" was never a girl to be satisfied with merely a good start. At the end of one year, she took a stenographic position with a large printing firm whose work was largely among advertisers. It was there that she came in contact, for the first time, with her future profession.

The stenographer budded into secretary for one of the firm's executives. Taking his dictation, answering his telephone calls, making his appointments gave her daily opportunity to see what the field of advertising really was. If he was working with a business man who wished to have a catalog printed, she saw the "copy" come in, pages of description of this article and that. She saw the illustrations for the catalog arrive— photographs or pen and ink pictures. Often she looked over the shoulders of the "lay-out" man, watching him as he decided upon the size of the illustration on the printed page, and just where it should be placed. Minna Hall Carothers—her name was Minna Hall Simmons then—was a secretary and she was using her secretaryship to learn everything possible about what passed through her hands.

She learned to good purpose. From secretary, she was promoted to the position of estimator and purchaser of the paper for the catalogs which her printing firm got out. And she came to know, as every advertising woman must know, just what kinds of paper may best be used for this purpose or that—paper that was strong, not easily to be torn; fine paper which by its very

finish gave distinction to the catalog; dull, rough
paper that was sometimes preferable to smooth
and glossy paper.

Having scrutinized costs and paper so thor-
oughly, once more she began to look about her
for something new to learn. And she saw advertising agencies, where all kinds of advertisements
for magazines, billboards, and newspapers were
prepared. The idea of doing this work attracted
her. So Minna Hall Carothers entered such an
agency, there to learn every branch, and they are
many, of advertising work. She bought space—
that is, she decided in which magazines and which
papers certain advertisements should appear—
and having decided, negotiated with the magazines and papers, sending them the advertisements in question. Later she wrote copy, describ-
ing in colorful words the articles to be advertised.
She became head of a department which took the
illustrations prepared by the artists, which took
the copy as prepared by the copy-writers and decided the size of the type, the size of the illustrations and, in short, saw the whole advertisement
through to its published end. Then the war came
along and changed everything. It changed Mrs.
Carothers' work. She became advertising manager for a concern engaged in the manufacture
of analine dye-stuffs.

"How exciting!" said I.

"Very!" said she. "About that time German

dyes were excluded from this country. American dyes had to be developed. Imagine being advertising manager in such a place—waiting for the chemists to perfect some new process, learning just what that process was and why it was of use in the new dye and hurrying back to my office to describe it all for the mills who were to use it!"

But dye-stuffs could not hold her indefinitely. For an interval she ran the Minna Hall Carothers Service Agency. Then she turned to selling. And today she is associated with the Powers Reproduction Corporation, where she sells to advertisers themselves the photo-engraving services of her company.

"When I was holding down my first job," she told me, "the firm used to say, 'Too bad you aren't a man, so that we could send you out to sell.' It never dawned on me at that time that selling was possible for a young woman. I? Sell? The idea was preposterous! But now I am able to say, with confidence, that it is a knowledge of my field which counts and my ability to sell. And I am not handicapped because I happen to be a woman instead of a man."

I was eager to know why she, who has had so much experience, prefers selling to managing an advertising agency, or to copywriting, or buying space.

"Because it is never monotonous. Because it

takes me out-of-doors. Because I go out to all kinds of people in all kinds of businesses. Because there is a thrill in not knowing what you are going to come up against. Because there is a thrill in overcoming difficult situations, in getting a customer's name on the stern dotted line. And because—should I mention it—selling pays most generously. Yes, at last I have come through to the work that I prefer.

"But don't think that all my advertising experience is not useful to me now. My work today is intimately concerned with advertising. I go to advertisers of many kinds and endeavor to sell them the engraving services of my concern. In order to prove to them that we can produce their work satisfactorily, I must know what they wish to accomplish. If I can give them helpful suggestions, so much the better. They then realize that we will do more for them than handle the mechanical process of getting out their engraving. We will give them personal interest and service which will be useful to them in securing better business results. In order to do this, I must constantly study my prospective customers' advertising problems. And this is another reason why I like what I am doing—I am always learning something new and interesting."

The typewriters clicked. Sunlight poured through a large window. Copies of colored advertisements, for which photo-engravings had been made by the Powers Reproduction Corporation, looked at us from four walls.

"You are a woman," I said, "and you are in advertising. Tell me what you think of the field for girls."

"Girls and advertising? Women have as definite a place in advertising as men. You find them buying space, buying art work, writing copy, laying out advertisements, selling space or buying and selling engravings. It all depends on each girl and what she is fitted to do. In advertising, just as in everything else, a girl must discover herself. And she can discover herself in advertising by getting a job in advertising and trying herself out.

"Young women, as well as men, can study products and plan advertisements which will tell others about those products in an interesting and compelling way. In fact with some products. I think many young women have a natural advantage. I am thinking of advertisements which describe foods or clothing. A young woman is apt to know what other women will wish to hear about food and clothes. If it's a new cake flour, whether it saves time in mixing or gives an especially delicious taste to the finished cake. If it's a dress, what the distinctive points are of its style or its material. For products such as this, young women have the advantage of a background of experience."

"Do young women, then, succeed everywhere in the advertising world?" I asked.

Mrs. Carothers hesitated. "They *could* succeed everywhere," she said after a moment, "depending upon each one's own ability. Men, at least the men higher up, are fair in giving you a chance to show what you can do. Of course, if you are inexperienced and obstinate, you deserve a little prejudice."

I wanted to talk with her about women in business and men in business and both in business together. I wanted to talk with her about women executives who are fair and big and splendid, about men executives who are fair and big and splendid—and about women executives who are not and men executives who are not.

But looking at her, I knew what she would reply: "Everything depends upon the person." And in any case, she had judiciously summed up the whole situation. Women in business are not there for favors. If they demand the same business advantages as men, they must accept the same disadvantages. The finest advertising women know this—or most of them. They accept the hazards gallantly. They want to get on. They work long hours when long hours are necessary. They stick to it like Trojans. They tackle big jobs.

"Girls who think advertising means an easy life should stay out of it." Mrs. Carothers was not mincing her words. "There is a prevalent idea that advertising is copy-writing and nothing else. It's a wrong idea. Copy-writing is only a small part of this highly diversified work. I asked a hundred advertising women, once, about the work which each was doing. Fewer than twenty-five of them wrote copy."

She talked on with quiet authority. How would she go about it if she were today starting on her advertising career? She would go to college if she could possibly afford it, choosing one of those colleges where courses in advertising are offered —and there are now over one hundred and fifty such colleges in this country. But she would not limit her studies to advertising—no, indeed! She would enter the English department, especially the writing courses. She would study psychology, to add to her knowledge of people. And, in between, she would sandwich as many other courses as she was able.

"Because a wide range of information is invaluable to work in advertising.

"But if I couldn't go to college," she continued, "I would get any possible position in an advertising agency or in the advertising department of a store or other concern that has an advertising office. Any possible job I could get—file clerk, stenographer, anything so that papers would pass through my hands and I could see what was going on. Preferably, I think, stenographer. In my own experience, stenography was the opening wedge. They would not have taken me in that office if I had not had it. On the other hand, it was necessary for me to pull myself away from it after I had gained sufficient experience and had some idea of what I wished to do. Being a good stenographer or secretary can in time become a handicap as well as having been an opening wedge. Your employer may wish to keep you right where you are indefinitely, because you are so useful to him.

"And there is another point to be remembered. Stenographic or filing positions are, in certain circumstances, no opening wedge at all. A girl must determine for herself whether she is acquiring experience which is actually leading her into the field of advertising, or wherever she wishes to go, or whether she is in a blind alley. My stenographic position happened to give me great opportunity to learn the mechanics of advertising. Some stenographic positions are blind alleys, nothing more."

I asked Mrs. Carothers about the actual writing of advertisements.

"Suppose," she replied, "that I was working in an advertising agency, where all kinds of advertisements are prepared, and was given a tooth paste advertisement. Suppose it was a new product on the market. In all probability, the art department, the research department and the

copy writer would hold an august conference.
The art department would make suggestions for
the pictures of the product—of the package or
of the tube or of a presentation of the paste in
actual use. The research department would sub-
mit data as to the other tooth pastes on the
market, the needs and desires of the public in
the matter of tooth paste and a list of the facts
concerning this particular tooth paste which the
manufacturer wished to emphasize in his advertising campaign.

"With all this in mind, I would then go off by
myself and puzzle over that tooth paste. I would
think of the people who would use it and just
what it is in a tooth paste that most appeals to
them—its taste, its possibilities for cleanliness,
its container. You know what you think of when
you change from the tooth paste you have been
using to a new one. I would not depend upon
my own experience alone. I would talk with my
friends about their tooth pastes, and different
kinds of friends, to get all points of view. In
planning the kind of advertisement to use, it
would also be necessary for me to remember how
much money the tooth paste concern wished to
spend, and whether the advertisement itself was
to appear in magazines or in street cars or on billboards. What is effective in one is often not effective in another. And at last, after my pondering,
an original idea for that tooth paste advertise-

ment would break into being. The slogan *Four out of Five* was conceived by a copy writer who looked at tooth paste and pondered."

I thought of the advertisements I read every day, in magazines and newspapers, on billboards and in trolley cars. And suddenly I saw, back of each one, the copy-writers, the artists, the layout workers, the printers, the managers and the secretaries.

"But advertising is never," said this astute business woman, "easy."

I knew she spoke the unvarnished truth.

"Then, Mrs. Carothers, your advice is——?"

"Advertise!"

NEYSA McMEIN

A girl
who liked to
draw and paint

NEYSA McMEIN

VERMILION, and violet, and cobalt blue.
. . . Ochre and a dab of shiny black.
. . . Every color known to painters was in
vivid evidence all over Neysa McMein's studio—
labelled neatly in tubes, smeared in oily profusion
on her palette, and taking human form in a half-
finished portrait of Beatrice Lillie, the actress,
which stood full length on an upright canvas. I
was almost certain that Neysa in her blue smock
had, in a moment of deviltry, broken up the rain-
bow into its component hues and spilled them
lavishly over the room. I was almost certain. . . .
Anyway, there was the room, and there was the
color, and there was Neysa McMein.

"Come in," said the blue smock. Of course it
may have been the artist who spoke, but it
sounded like her blue smock. Voices can have
color, as well as palettes, and this voice was un-
deniably a cerulian blue.

I advanced into the big studio, liked it immediately, liked its owner, and sat down in one of its chairs. That was a feat of dexterity, for the room was a delicious jumble of everything comfortable and everything colorful. It was like a curio shop, though much nicer. There were brushes—big fellows, built for use. There was a tall skylight, built for sun. There were the innumerable originals of magazine covers which Neysa McMein has painted. There were vases, bric-a-brac, photographs, and a table on which reposed a bitten-into piece of toast. There was the top of Joan Whitney's head, visible above two canvasses. There was the half-finished Beatrice Lillie. And as a surprise, for this was a painter's studio, there were two pianos and a collection of musical instruments!

"Before we begin," I said, "I want to get your name straight. Is the 'McMein' pronounced with an *a* sound or an *i* sound?"

Neysa McMein laughed heartily. "*A,*" she said. "My name was never known to be pronounced correctly or spelled correctly. The worst blunder though, was made by a man, once who called me in an interview, 'Mr. Neuter McNeil!' "

It was my turn to laugh now. It was singularly easy to laugh in this room. Again my eyes went on an adventure. Raw sienna, lemon yellow, Chinese red . . . and over in the corner, a gorgeous green. . . . My eyes came back to

Neysa McMein, well-known artist and illustrator.

And because she was human and very much herself, Miss McMein was the most vivid thing in a vivid room. She is a woman not difficult to look upon, a paintable woman. Two things impressed me: her low-in-the-back hair which tries to be gold and then decides, rather reluctantly, to be plain brown with a sprinkling of gray; and her long slim legs which end, charmingly, in high-heeled slippers. Did I say two things? Three! Big gray eyes.

"Did you study art at an art school?" I asked.

"Yes. At the Chicago Art Institute. Not for long—I couldn't afford more. But long enough to get the beginnings."

And she told me the story. Neysa McMein, though at the time she had not adopted her present name, left the Chicago Art Institute to take a position in a millinery house. She needed money. It was "hack work," but it taught the novice her trade. Drawing hats for a millinery house is not art. But it is a type of commercial illustration which may lead somewhere else. And Neysa drew hat shapes. She learned perspective, line, proportion. She learned accuracy. Crowns, brims, trimming—from morning till night she made them into pictures.

"When I drew a hat wrong," said Miss McMein, "I had to draw it over again. That's the only way you can learn to draw good hats. That's the only way you can learn to draw anything. Just as later when I started to paint women's faces and put crossed-eyes into their heads, I had to do the eyes over and over until they got straight. What could have been finer training? Hats, hats, hats! In the end, I could draw them with my eyes shut."

A large Persian cat leaped into her lap, snuggled its head under Miss McMein's chin and purred so boisterously that I could hear the rumble six feet away. She patted the shaggy fur and went on talking:

"And then I took to the stage. It was stock. I came to New York, played awhile and got out."

"But why did you get out? You liked the stage, didn't you?"

The answer was in the true McMein manner. It was short, colloquial and to the point. "I was no good," she said.

And that, incidentally, is a strong piece in Neysa McMein's armor. She is honest in her self-criticism. She hasn't a single illusion about Neysa McMein. When she is experimenting in her work and finds that she cannot do a thing well, she admits it. And either gives it up or sets to work to improve her technique.

"But get this straight," she said, and smiled a little at her prominence as a magazine-cover artist and a painter of portraits. "I'm not in any sense contributing to contemporary art. I didn't study long enough. I don't know the fundamentals. That's why I'm stumped every now and then and have to work my fingers off in getting a good likeness. Why, I'm stumped right now on Beatrice Lillie!"

I looked at the half-finished actress and protested. As far as my amateur eyes could make out, this was the very Beatrice Lillie who convulses an audience—and me—with her antics. But Neysa McMein was working for something I didn't see.

The rest of her story came quickly. When she left the stock company, she resumed her commercial art. She painted pastels for magazine covers, in New York City because more magazines are published there than in any other city in our country. And she went from art editor to art editor selling her wares.

"It took a lot of shoe leather and a lot of time. But I must say I like editors! Why shouldn't I? They bought my pictures then, they buy my pictures now. Of course, perhaps I was so persistent that they became exhausted and took my stuff to get rid of me!"

Perhaps. But I was not convinced. I knew that, despite her joking, Neysa McMein has not got to her present place through casual chance. Things don't happen that way. Eventually the talented win recognition and the half-talented drop back. But she has studied hard and she has worked hard.

And she will continue to study hard and to work hard as long as she paints. Because she has had special talent, she has been recognized. But the talent has not done away with the necessity for study and work. Neysa McMein believes that an artist has no right to a temperament, nor to coddling, that she should learn to work anywhere, any time. She herself has, furthermore, excellent health and a willingness to take infinite pains with her work.

"But I am not a *real* artist," she declared again. "I belong to those whose artistic ability is turned to the producing of something which is wanted by the public and so is immediately salable."

I knew what she meant. She was thinking of such artists as Cecilia Beaux, an eminent contemporary painter, who has already had an exhibition of her work in the Metropolitan Museum. She was thinking of those artists whose pictures will live for generations, who have painted the great pictures of the world. Such artists wish to express a spiritual thing, an ideal through their work, painting solely for the purpose of catching on their canvas some intangible beauty.

"I didn't study long enough even to try to paint in that way," went on Miss McMein. "There is nothing to take the place of study—study—study if you wish to be an artist."

I spoke of girls who like to draw and paint and who wish to become artists. She was interested at once. "The best thing you can do is to enter a good art school," she said. "A *good* art school. A place like the Chicago Art Institute is always glad to tell you which schools are good and where they are. Such a school takes money but it's worth it. It does two things for you. It trains what ability you have, and you may have a great deal, and it helps you to find out just where in the field of art you will fit in.

"If, when you get out, you want to go on with *real* painting,"—and once more I knew what Neysa McMein meant by that—"you must make up your mind that you have years and years and years of work ahead of you, painting and painting and painting. You may get recognition quickly. You probably won't. Most artists don't. And while you are working, you will have to eat. So, to support yourself, you may take on a certain amount of commercial work such as illustrating magazine stories or books or drawing for advertisements. A good many artists do this.

"If, on the other hand, you decide to be a commercial artist, there are any number of places that use commercial art. Beside magazine and book illustration, there are the fashion concerns

that must have artists to draw their style designs.
Wall-paper manufacturers who want to have
wall-paper designs made. Textile manufacturers
and many others.

"Sometimes artists are on the regular paid
staffs of these concerns. Sometimes they work as
what are called 'free lance' artists, which means
they don't get a salary and don't have a steady
position. They go from concern to concern, obtaining what commissions they can. It is uncertain, but many artists prefer it because of its
variety."

Copyists, draftsmen, commercial etchers,
poster painters—their name is legion. "Yes, if
a girl likes to draw or paint and if she has learned
how to do it well, she can find an opening in commercial work in our cities," declared Neysa Mc-
Mein. "And if commercial work in a manufacturing plant or a publishing house or a store
doesn't appeal to her, she can teach art in the
public schools. A good many normal schools
have art courses and courses in how to teach art,
too." And always, there is the possibility for the
few, of becoming great artists.

"But don't forget," she concluded with a
laugh, "to be a good saleswoman. The time I
have spent studying out just what would fit into
this magazine or that—and then going and telling them so! I believe it's what teachers of sales-
manship call attracting the attention, arousing

the interest, creating the desire and closing the sale. Well, whatever it is, I like to do it. I like to sell my own work. I would like to sell other things, too.

"Yes, I went into illustrating to support myself and I have. But remember this—I enjoy illustrating. I have never been sorry I started doing it. And it hasn't all been easy, either."

She told me of her own struggles and of those of her artist friends, of the disappointment when a picture is rejected after many weeks, even years, of work upon it, of the blow it is when an artist has counted upon the sale of that picture for her livelihood. She told me of the frequent difficulty of obtaining the kind of work you, as an artist, really wish to do even in the commercial field.

"But it's better now than it ever has been. All the advertising that is being done means more commercial art work. And more commercial art means that artists can earn a living with their particular ability. And certainly that's better than having to drop it altogether."

"There are other things that I'd like to try," she went on, after a pause. "Music, for instance."

So that was the explanation of two pianos and many musical instruments in her studio!

"But since I can't earn my living by it, I make it my hobby."

She is a happy person. She delights in her studio, her Persian angora, her orgy of brilliant paints, her two pianos—and in her baby and her husband. When I put the question to her, she assured me that the husband and the very young daughter in no way interfere with her painting.

But—"Oh, she's lovely!" said the mother, and I knew that Neysa McMein would unhesitatingly put away her profession if it interfered with that baby.

"I am going to buy her a new doll this afternoon," she told me.

CHARLOTTE COWDREY BROWN

*A girl
who loved
growing things*

CHARLOTTE COWDREY BROWN

"**M**ANY girls," said Charlotte Cowdrey Brown, "have an innate love of growing things."

We were sitting in her rarely appointed drawing room. Gray velvet, a paisley shawl, a vase full of blush roses, exotic candlesticks—but the sky was shut out and the March wind. Through a subtle communication, I knew that Mrs. Brown was sorry. I could imagine her puttering around hollyhocks and blue larkspur. I could imagine a spade in her capable hands.

Charlotte Cowdrey Brown's grandfather was English-born and that, she thinks, explains her love of flowers. She has always loved them. As a little girl, she was fascinated with the family gardens, begging for one of her own until at last it was given to her. She took her garden very seriously. She asked innumerable questions of those who had planted in their gardens what she was planning for hers.

Nor did her enthusiasm wane with the appearance of the first green shoots. All through the summer, she tended her flowers. And the flowers responded. Charlotte's first garden was a lovely one, even though it was not uniformly what the young gardener had hoped.

By the time she was thirty her flower gardens were many. On the coast of New Jersey, she developed a blue garden, a yellow garden, a pink garden and, most beautiful of all, a snow-white garden. Flowers grew and thrived under her care. Each plant was an individual to her, a living thing unlike any other. And flower colors were her specialty.

It is not surprising, then, that other women wished to know of her methods. She became a lecturer on flowers. She wrote a book called *Color in the Garden*. For twenty years she has been an active member of the Farm and Garden Association.

"It's horrid to have to live in the city," said Charlotte Cowdrey Brown. "I miss my gardens so.

"But I enjoy my lecturing," she continued. "It is a real delight to me to exchange gardening experiences with other flower lovers. I never return from a lecture trip without having learned something new. And I like, too, to tell young women what I know of agriculture as a field for them. For the girl who loves to make things grow, who has plenty of patience and who is strong, agriculture has its great appeal."

"Then women are at work in it?" I asked.

"Yes, especially in such forms of it as truck gardening, keeping bees, dairying, poultry farming or growing flowers. Contrary to what many still think, farm work is not too difficult for the young woman who has excellent health. Dr. Dudley Sargent declared, after employing twenty-five women on his farm, that if a girl is robust she can do every farm chore without injury to her health. Mrs. Edward Parker Davis, who owns and runs a stock farm of one hundred and thirty-two acres, says she find that young women make the best farm hands. Girls are refusing to be delicate. Heavy manual labor no longer appalls the strong young woman who wishes to work out-of-doors. And I often come across one who is engaged in a surprising occupation. An Oregon woman, a timber cruiser, once told me that her long trips on foot and on horseback were positively pleasant and that she recommended forestry as a possibility for women.

"I know women who have bought farms for themselves and who have proceeded to run them. I know women who have inherited farms and who have decided to go on with them. The ones who have succeeded are those who have had thorough knowledge of the work, enough money to employ help, to buy necessary equipment, to tide their own living expenses over poor seasons and who, as I said, have had good health, patience and persistence. For it does take patience and it does take persistence. So much is out of your control, you see—frost and rain and drought. The courage of even the staunchest-hearted is often sorely tried. Edna Ferber's interesting story, *So Big,* gives a most understanding picture of what it means to a woman to run a farm.

"It is important for every farmer to know scientific methods of farming. Some of the women whom I know have been able to take a course in one of the excellent agricultural schools of the country. Others, unable to spend the time or the money in this, have added to their own farming experience by studying such reliable publications as those issued by the Department of Agriculture in Washington and by attending farm institutes where authorities on various phases of farming lecture and demonstrate.

"No," continued Mrs. Brown earnestly, "it is never easy. Beside the difficulties of contending with the soil and uncertain weather, there are those of marketing your produce, once you have grown it. There are the difficulties of obtaining not only sufficient help but help of the right kind.

"But because the work itself appeals to them, because they can live in the country and spend most of their time out-of-doors, women are persisting in it."

And I listened to the stories of two girls who have persisted. The first was that of a girl whose father was a professor in the agricultural school of a college. While she was still in high school, she said to her father one day, "I want a cow of my own."

Her father looked at her curiously and replied, "A cow is a great deal of work."

"I know," said the girl, "but I want one. If you will let me have one of yours, I will pay you for it with the profits on the milk."

Because his daughter was so deeply in earnest and because the professor realized that she already knew a great deal about the care of a cow, he fell in with her plan. The girl went about her self-appointed work in a thorough way. She gave time and thought to her cow. She read all she could find on the subject of her feeding. She consulted with her father and other owners of cows on the various problems that arose. And she enjoyed it all so much, it was not long before she was announcing that as soon as she completed her schooling she meant to have a dairy of her own.

Today she has that dairy—with her husband, who is a graduate of the agricultural school in which her father is a professor. She herself oversees her share of all work that is done and declares that it is no less interesting, even though more strenuous, than the care of her first cow.

The other story was one of great courage. In

an agricultural school just before the war, a young man and a young woman studied side by side. They were specializing in poultry farming, both having already had some experience in it. And as they talked together of what they would do when they completed their study, they came to realize that the happiest future which could await them would be one which they should live together. And they became engaged.

Then the war came and the young man went away. When he returned, he was blind. The young woman loved him—and formulated a plan. When she suggested it to him, he was reluctant. But there was in her a great courage and a belief in their own powers.

"Why not have a chicken farm?" she asked. "You know as much as you ever did about the work. And I am strong. We'll be partners!"

In time, she persuaded him and they were married. The story of their steady struggle to establish their chicken business is a long one. It was necessary for them to borrow money. The first farm which they bought proved an unwise purchase. But today they have their chicken farm on a main automobile thoroughfare. A sign which hundreds of people pass daily heralds the fact of their fresh eggs and chickens for sale. Their scientific training and their real skill in conducting their poultry raising have brought a deserved reputation for excellence to their eggs and chickens.

By the roadside itself, the two have built a small shop where they sell sandwiches and soft drinks, with chicken sandwiches their specialty. The young woman's mother is in charge of the shop, which not only adds to the family's income but is also a means for marketing the eggs and chickens.

The mortgage on the little farm is gradually being paid off. And the enterprise is establishing itself as a successful venture. To be sure, the two have been helped by people's special interest in them. Nevertheless, the chief factor in their work has been their intelligence and their skill.

"The growing of flowers appeals to many women," went on Mrs. Brown. "Some have their own greenhouses. Others act as assistants. Flower farms ship their tea roses or their yellow primroses or their peonies or their double violets to wholesale and individual florists.

"Drug-growing has much in common with flower-growing and may be made profitable under intelligent direction. You may specialize in a wide variety, in ginseng or digitalis (a heart stimulant), in golden seal, in spigelia or others. A woman in Delaware has a sassafras farm. A woman in the South cultivates Oriental poppies.

"Women who have no money for launching

a more ambitious enterprise or who must work in the vicinity of their own homes are developing special outdoor projects. Some are excellent seedsmen. They are specializing in many kinds— in sweet William (Newport pink), Colorado columbine, zinnia seeds or something equally sought after.

"I know one woman who has turned her front yard into rare white petunias and is selling the seeds wholesale. There is great demand for selected colors. Seed growers who cultivate one color—say, lavender—weeding out every other color, are finding that these selected seeds bring a higher price.

"There is no reason why girls cannot undertake work with seeds. A group of Girl Scouts in Oregon were interested in the preservation of wild flowers. They became acquainted with the spots near their home town where these flowers grew. And then a plan occurred to them. Why not gather and sell wildflower seeds?

"They marked the places, returning to gather the seeds with the help of a local gardener. Carefully labelling each packet, they sold them widely. Today they proudly tell their friends of a Scotch garden in which their wildflower seeds have been planted.

"Some very clever selling ideas have been evolved by women who are conducting special enterprises. Often to these ideas no less than to their abilty as gardeners or poultry raisers, is due their financial success. A Kentucky woman who advertises "True Heavenly Blue Morning Glory Seeds" sells them for five cents a seed. A woman in New Jersey specializes in cranberries —"as big as cherries." She wraps them attractively, ties them with red ribbon and sells them as Christmas presents.

"A woman in Vermont uses the picturesque story of her vegetable dyes to good advantage in her selling. This woman grows her own flax and makes her own dyes. Her vegetable dyes are made from goldenrod and seaweed and the juice of black walnuts. She pours the dye into clear glass bottles, leaves the bottles on a snow-bank all winter and calls the color permanent if it has retained its original intensity until the spring thaw. Then she weaves her dyed flax into a beautiful design and finds that women enjoy possessing the colorful article made in so unusual a way."

I asked Mrs. Brown what suggestion she would give a girl who, like herself, is interested in growing things.

She smiled. "Look around, first of all," she said. "I haven't even mentioned all the possibilities. Architects are employing young women as landscape architects who have made a special study of the work of effectively laying out trees and bushes and gardens for the grounds surrounding homes.

Here and there a tree nursery is run by a woman —and there are schools of forestry in various of our universities where the ways of trees are to be learned.

"Agricultural experiment stations employ young women who are grounded in science in general and in biology in particular to study such problems as soil care, animal breeding, crop rotation, plant diseases and insect pests, and to help prepare bulletins giving their findings to those interested. Public schools where garden work is carried on employ a supervisor for this department.

"Yes, look around. But—have a garden! Plant flowers or vegetables. Or raise chickens. Or a pig. Or a cow. Know the fun and the interest of it while you are young and it may even point the way to what you will wish to have as your ultimate vocation.

"Girls today have many opportunities to experiment in this out-of-door work in school or in camp, or through such organizations as the boys' clubs and girls' clubs of the Department of Agriculture in Washington. Any girl who is interested in planning her garden scientifically can obtain a wealth of information in the pamphlets of the Department of Agriculture, a list of which will be sent her upon request. It is surprising what girls have accomplished through these tomato clubs and corn clubs and pig clubs and canning clubs. Exhibits of their work at county fairs are of highest excellence.

"If, later, a girl decides that she is interested in entering professionally some phase of this out-of-door work, I would suggest that she inform herself concerning the courses given in agricultural schools, as well as the requirements for entrance into these schools. She should also inquire into the kinds of opportunity which will in all probability be open to her when she is graduated from the agricultural school.

"To grow anything well," said Mrs. Brown, gazing reflectively at the blush roses on the table, "you must know so much about it. With my flower gardens, I must know flower habits and flower requirements. I need a thorough understanding, based on experience and reading, of the kind of soil, the amount of sun and the length of exposure or shelter which each flower needs.

"Each must be tended as carefully as a child. Although—" and Mrs. Brown laughed gleefully, "flowers certainly have this advantage. If a child proves a disappointment, care and responsibility are still your lot. But if a flower proves fractious, you can pull it up and throw it over the fence!"

I mingled my laughter with hers. Sitting there in her lovely drawing room, it was far easier for me to think of her puttering around that white garden down in New Jersey than as a city woman. It was easier to think of her among banks of bridal wreath, and top-heavy snowballs, and pale sweet peas, and white petunias, and love-in-a-mist, and luxurious laurel, and candytuft, and sweet alyssum, and delicate mignonette, and lilies of the valley hiding in their leaves, and white orchises and saxifrage and sweet white trillium. . .

EDNA WATSON BAILEY

*A girl
who chose teaching
first of all*

EDNA WATSON BAILEY

A CROWD of girls and boys rushed by, into the next room. But Eloise sat in her little chair.

The sunshine, streaming through the wide-open window behind her, alighted upon her yellow hair and made dancing gold of it. Quietly, Eloise listened to the noisy fun in the other room. Her deep blue eyes did not stir from the doorway, as though she were wishing for nothing more than to be in there with the girls and the boys.

Yet she did not move. Her small hands folded upon the lap of her blue smocked dress, she sat where she was all morning. She sat there when the teacher called, "Lunch time," and the boys and the girls scurried away. She was sitting there when her mother came for her at three o'clock.

Rather, ten minutes after three. For Eloise's mother was stopped by the teacher, in the hall.

And for ten minutes the two talked earnestly together.

"Come, dear," said Eloise's mother, kissing her gently. "Time to go home." Obediently, Eloise got up from the little chair and walked to the cloak room where she found her coat and hat hanging on the low peg above which was pasted the picture of the girl in the pony cart. Eloise had noticed that picture when she hung up her coat—so, now, she knew right where her coat and hat were to be found.

At home, Grandmother fluttered to the door. "And what did my darling do, her first day at school?" she asked.

Eloise looked up from out the deep-blue eyes. "I sat in a chair," she said.

"She did," admitted Eloise's mother when later she and Grandmother were alone. "She just sat, every blessed minute of the day."

"Do you mean to tell me that that Miss Dunbar we've been hearing so much about let her stay there, like that?"

Eloise's mother nodded.

"What will she do tomorow, then?"

"Let her sit," smiled Eloise's mother. "I am afraid you don't get the idea, mother. You know that Eloise is the least assertive of the three girls, don't you? And you must realize how rarely she has any suggestions of her own about what they shall do. She follows the lead of the other two, even though they are younger. This is her chance to be herself—to have plans of her own, and to follow those plans. If Miss Dunbar takes her by the hand and leads her about now, Eloise will not become—well, Eloise."

Grandmother sniffed.

She sniffed again when, the next afternoon, Eloise's reply to her fluttery question was the same. "I sat," said Eloise succinctly.

"And she had *no lunch*," added Grandmother, accusingly, to Eloise's father when he was given the story of it after the children's bedtime.

"If she doesn't know enough to go where the lunch is, when she has been told, I give up," replied Eloise's father.

For three days, Eloise sat in the little chair. For three days, her blue eyes burned deep, as she watched the doorway through which came tumultuous sounds of busy enjoyment.

On the morning of the fourth day, when the children were at work on a fire-house, Eloise quietly slid from the little chair and crossed the room. From the doorway, she peered onto the floor where the children were so absorbingly occupied. The teacher, at a far window, was reading a book. No one paid the slightest attention to Eloise. She took one step into the room and stood there, a long while, deep blue eyes on the rising fire-house. Then she walked over and picked up a pointed block.

"Here," she said, holding it out to the Boy nearest.

"Put it on yourself," replied the Boy.

That afternoon, as she and her mother approached home, Eloise dropped her mother's hand and ran up the steps of the porch.

"Oh, Grandmother!" she cried, the blue eyes glinting sparks of excitement. "I helped build a fire-house."

Grandmother kissed her. "And did you have lunch?" asked she. But Eloise was hurrying upstairs to the play-room.

"For the girl who knows and loves children, teaching is a wonderful work," said Dr. Edna Bailey. "Think of the interest of it! A roomful of children, every one different from every other one. You are to be with them every school day. Teaching them? The word 'teaching' falls far short of what you really do. Rather, you are their guide, pointing out to them fascinating trails which they themselves may take. And along those trails, you are helping them to discover a world of interesting things.

"And how children do like to learn! Sometimes I think it is their chief characteristic. It is as natural for them as flying is natural for young robins. Physics? Teach a boy physics with his own radio and he is so excited that he will forget to grudge the time spent in study—because he is learning something that he wants to know. Zoölogy? As a catalog of long names, it frightens a child away. But zoölogy meaning a child's pets, and the animals in the nearby zoo—how enthralling!"

I had come to Dr. Edna Bailey because a man who knows many of the eighty-five thousand women teachers in this country today had told me of her splendid work as head of the department of sciences in the University High School, University of California. He had said the boys and girls in Dr. Bailey's classes eagerly look forward to them, actually sorry when the bell rings for the close of each session.

I found a woman glad that she is a teacher, preferring teaching to any other profession. It was not surprising. You cannot do work as she has done it without enjoying it. Immediately, I responded to the gleam of comradeship in her eyes—comradeship not for me alone, but for all the world, great enough, I knew, to give each boy, each girl, no matter how cantankerous, a special welcoming. Dr. Bailey, tall, prepossessing, looks like a mother, acts like a mother, and turns out to be the teacher-mother of two young daughters. A very wise mother.

"My life," she said, in answer to my question, "has not been startling. I was born in West Virginia; I grew up in Tennessee and Missouri; and I went, eventually, through eight years of training at the University of California, leading to the degree of Doctor of Philosophy in 1910.

"Every girl's early years give her something distinctive because she lives them just as she does. My moving from one part of the country to another gave me adaptability. I came to know many kinds of people and the various ways in which they liked to live. I always enjoyed meeting new people. Perhaps it was this interest in people, especially in those younger than I, which led me to teaching. At any rate, teaching was the only thing which I considered doing. And, today, I never tire of the young folks in our High School. If only I had time to tell you about some of them and what they are doing now that they have been graduated!"

Boys and girls—growing up—remembering Dr. Edna Bailey, her friendliness, what she taught them from books, from life—grateful to her for it. "Surely," I thought, "a teacher's reward is far, far more than the salary she receives."

"Time was," went on Dr. Bailey, "when teaching was almost the only occupation which welcomed young women. The result was that many girls entered it because they were forced to earn their own living, not because they wished to become teachers. Today, this is changing. I welcome the opportunities girls have to go into many kinds of work, for it means—besides the fact that they may now find work suited to their taste—

that, more and more, only those will become teachers to whom children or young people and the teaching of a congenial subject have a real appeal. This gives us happier teachers and happier children. No longer, when a girl happens to be bookish, do we invariably exclaim 'She was made to be a teacher.' Isn't that significant?"

Another point occurred to me. "I had never before thought of it in just this way," I said. "But is there any other profession in which a young woman may choose to be associated with those of the age which most appeals to her?"

Dr. Bailey smiled. "Almost none! The girl who enjoys small children may become a kindergarten teacher, or go into one of the nursery schools for those still younger. There are not many nursery schools as yet, but they are coming. If she enjoys children of elementary school age, she may enter there.

"Of course," she added, with great good-humor, "I think my job is, of all teaching jobs, the nicest. I do enjoy boys and girls of high school age. They are old enough to show real intelligence, but not so old that they are 'set' in their ways. It is remarkable how wisely they manage their own affairs when the school authorities give them half a chance. And I enjoy the sciences, oh! so much."

I remembered a teacher of my own who enjoyed the sciences "oh, so much!" The quiet woods, today, teem with fascinating life for me because of that teacher.

"And that is another thing for the girl to consider who is thinking of teaching. She may teach the subject which has greatest appeal to her— provided, of course, she goes on to secure adequate training in it. If she enjoys books and her work in high school English, she may wish to specialize in English in college, later teaching it. So, too, with history. With any subject. If she enjoys home tasks, if she likes to cook, she may wish to become a domestic science teacher. If she likes to make things, manual training is a possibility, or music, if she is musical. Or the other arts.

"If she has special aptitude for it—and a great deal of patience—she may assume teaching responsibility in those classes for backward children which so many communities are fortunately organizing today. Some children are born slow. These special classes for them are a godsend in three ways—the children themselves are no longer pushed, they no longer hold back the brighter children, and the teacher's load is substantially lightened. There are special classes, too, for gifted children.

"The choice is unlimited. And what pleasant associations a teacher has!" Dr. Bailey's eyes were glowing. "The other teachers in her school, the educators from all parts of the country whom she meets at various conventions, the parents of her children—and the books with which she is surrounded. Since teachers are needed everywhere, a young woman may secure a position in some new part of the country, traveling there and during her vacations gaining still more fresh and enjoyable experiences at every hand.

"Nor would I forget the respect which a teacher is accorded. There is a new and ever-growing appreciation of teachers in this country. And it is good to be appreciated!

"All the while a teacher is at work, she is expressing what is deepest in her nature. She enters into the lives of children or young people—and from time immemorial this has appealed to women. And she is working out her creative ideas through her effort to make the subject which she teaches vital to her children."

"But the disadvantages?" I asked. I had heard so much about the disadvantages of teaching.

"They are not greater in teaching than in other professions," declared Dr. Bailey. "Every profession has them. Every occupation has them. They are part of living. I believe the reason we hear so much about them in connection with teaching is that there are so many teachers! But if you enjoy your work in anything, the disadvantages become relatively unimportant."

I mentioned those of which I had most frequently heard—long hours, heavy work, small pay, monotony. Dr. Bailey considered them, one by one.

"Long hours? From nine to three or four in the afternoon is much shorter than customary office hours. To be sure, much depends on the special situation of the teacher. Teachers in private schools usually live in the school and are often called upon for duties outside their classrooms. But sometimes those duties consist of attending a beautiful concert or a fine play! Whenever a teacher mentions to me the necessity for preparation of the next day's work, after she has finished her classes for the day, I think of the young lawyer who lives down my street and the bulging brief case he brings home with him each night.

"But Saturdays and Sundays are, ordinarily, whole holidays to the teacher. And the summer! No other profession, certainly, gives a young woman the entire summer as a vacation, with its opportunity for travel, for further study, for leisurely reading.

"Inordinately heavy work? Yes, in many communities too much is required of the teachers. On the other hand, I do feel that we have not been as clever as we might in devising ways for saving ourselves. In the matter of test papers, for instance, the pupils themselves may correct their own or each other's. This helps the pupils as well as saving yourself long hours of labor. After all, it is the pupil, not the teacher, who needs the education of correcting his mistakes.

"Monotonous? If a teacher's work is monotonous, I honestly feel it is largely her own fault. Monotonous when you are working with children or young people, every one different? Monotonous when new ways of teaching are being tried on every side today—and a teacher has only to look about her and read or study in one of the many summer school courses to have those ideas for her own and to try them in her own classroom? I refuse to admit the monotony!

"Underpaid? Yes, too often. But teachers' salaries are being increased. And will be increased still further, I feel, when we teachers work to improve the quality of our teaching and to make our communities realize the value of what we are doing."

It was difficult to hold Dr. Bailey to herself, to her own work. But I persisted. The University High School, I learned, is an adjunct of the University of California at Berkeley. It includes the seventh grade through the twelfth, a six year course. Any boy or girl in California is eligible to attend this school. Besides the regular teachers, each semester there are a number of student teachers, graduates of the University of California, who are given an opportunity, as part of the course which leads them to a teaching diploma, to teach in this school, thus putting their theory into practice.

"Training to be a teacher?" continued Dr. Bailey—irresistibly! "It is almost as varied as the kinds of teaching, it would seem. No girl who wishes to be a teacher is shut off from the opportunity of a normal school, for they are to be found everywhere. The length of the course varies from one, two, three to four years, with a lengthening of the shorter ones, year after year. In twenty-six states there are to be found today teachers' colleges, requiring a high school diploma for admission, and giving a course four years in length.

"Most secondary schools ask a college degree of their teachers. And a young woman who wishes to teach in a college or university will, of course, attend college, specializing there in the subject which she most desires to teach, and going on to graduate work and degrees.

"Which brings me to something that I should like to shout from the housetops! Let every girl who wishes to be a teacher obtain as much education as she possibly can, broad, general education which will enrich life for her as well as train her to teach something. And let her *live,* along the way, welcoming every opportunity she has to become intimately acquainted with children. The girl who has younger brothers and sisters is storing up for herself valuable knowledge should she become a teacher. The girl who borrows her small cousin or her neighbors' children for playtime is learning much that will be of later use to her. What matter if she in time becomes a teacher of high school young people, or college students? They were children once, and our psychologists are showing us how inextricably related are their childhood days to the quirks and the twists of their mature dispositions. Specialize in children!"

"You had your own, Dr. Bailey," I said.

"Yes, I married a physician the year after I finished my college course."

"And you kept on teaching?"

"For the first two years only. Then I left the profession for a few years, returning to it in 1916, in the University High School. My husband died in 1919."

Here, I thought, was a brave woman. For seven years she has been shouldering the weight of a small family which looks to her for support. But Dr. Bailey did not talk of courage. Teaching, to her, is a challenge, not a burden. Nor does she, for a moment, feel sorry for herself.

"You can imagine how thankful I was that I was trained for a profession and could step into it, at once, when the need arose. Too often, marriage itself is a goal to girls. They do not realize that they must go on developing, if they and their families would be happy. And what an asset in their marriage—even though they do not continue with work outside the home—is the realization that they are equipped to combat whatever circumstances may arise of financial necessity.

"Formerly, very few young women continued teaching after marriage. In some places married women, and especially married mothers, are still debarred from the public schools. But this is passing. Detroit is a notable exception. There the experiment is now being tried of urging all its teachers who marry to stay in the profession. School officials there say the plan works very well."

"What a world of good a teacher can do!" I cried.

"Please," protested this mother of two young daughters, "don't put it that way. Children hate 'being done good to' and I sympathize with them. Surely a child has a right to self-respect. Who am I to do good to a child? But coöperation is another thing. Offered wisely, it transforms the school for the children. It transforms the schoolroom for the teacher. Coöperation. It is a new day.

"Teachers are coming to realize that they need not be policemen to the young—*should* not be, in fact. How much more fun just to be friends and, as friends, to grow together! The children will help the teacher. The teacher will help the children.

"Have you been in the new kind of school? The school that does not say, 'We are preparing children for life,' but, 'This *is* life?' The school that uses everything around it, as well as what is in the class room—the parks, the streets, the stores? If schools are cut off from life, they become an artificial thing. But if they are not—! I could tell you of a class of girls who are learning child hygiene by assisting in a day nursery. I could tell you of manual training classes who have made bird houses for parks. I could tell you of high school students whose editing of their high school paper counts in their English work. Schools—living things."

Here was vision. Small wonder that Dr. Bailey's pupils think of her with gratitude. Teaching, to her, is not a plodding means of earning a necessary living. It is a noble, human task. When all teachers know children as she knows them, and love children as she loves them, and trust children as she trusts them, schoolrooms will attract children, and teachers, as never before.

"But a teacher is not always free!" I exclaimed.

"No," she replied, "too frequently communities clamp down, hostilely, upon their teachers. Very often they say in effect, 'These youngsters are bothering us. Take 'em off our hands for three-quarters of the day. Teach 'em to read and write and spell—oh, teach 'em anything!' And

they begrudge money spent for equipment which
would help make interesting days of tread-mill
ones.

"What can teachers do then? They can teach
their communities as well as the children. Help
the parents—who vote—to realize what they, the
teachers, are trying to accomplish. A school is
part of the community. It does its best work
when it uses the community, and the community
uses it. It remains for the teacher to make the
community understand."

"And when it does?"

"When it does—listen! There is a school where
the younger children keep pets in the back yard,
learning physiology, foods and many other
things by caring for them. Slightly older children
there learn their arithmetic by running the school
store, selling notebooks, pads, pencils and other
necessary school supplies. Being in a large city,
they use that city, going to the docks, the ferries,
the factories, the stores, the art galleries, the
museums, returning to write poems about what
they have seen, or with new understanding for the
clothes that they wear and the food that they eat.
The children in this school are not mere numbers.
Each child is an individual, a person, more interested in some things than in others, perhaps
selfish, or shy or bold. But a person and treated
as such. Think of the teachers in this school.
Lessons? No, *children*—and adventures with

them. Patience? Yes, the teachers there need plenty of it. Failures? They know those, too. But just as the children are experimenting with this and that and learning as they go, so the teachers in this school are experimenting with this and that way of teaching and learning as they go.

"It is the dawn of a new day."

The same week in which Dr. Bailey talked with me of teaching, Eloise, the self-reliant, was overheard by her mother to say to her younger sister—and her mother told me—"Now, Genevieve, there is no reason at all why you can't build your own house, if you put your blocks *this* way. See—Miss Dunbar showed me. Now *you* do it."

MARION SPRAGUE GILMORE

*A girl who started
to be a singer and became
a dietitian*

MARION SPRAGUE
GILMORE

WHAT a background: A ton of ripe olives, pies in profusion, breasts and breasts and breasts of chicken, a carload of little fat Brussels sprouts, raspberry sherbet in vats, and cake, cake, cake! But Marion Gilmore was unbewildered. This huge aluminum kitchen was her natural habitat. She is executive dietitian at the Pennsylvania Hotel in New York, one of the Statler chain of hotels, and the largest single hotel in the world.

But she wasn't always executive dietitian. Once she was a little girl in Swanton, Vermont, who loved to smell food, and eat food, and prepare food. Others, however, were less cordial to her enthusiasm. The cook, for instance. Somehow Mary objected to having a six-year-old under her feet in the kitchen, dabbling in the bread dough.

"Go away," said Mary. "You're bothering me."

"Apologize," said Charles Gilmore, the usually indulgent father. Marion said nothing at all.

She said nothing because she was thinking deeply. How could she get on the good side of Mary, and thereby win the privilege of stirring up bread, and cake, and pies? By flattering her, of course. By saying that her biscuits were simply galuptious—and then Marion knew what she was going to do! She rushed into the kitchen, intercepted Mary just as she drew a pan of red-hot biscuits from the oven, stood on her tip-toes, and kissed them! The next day there was a blister on her mouth. But there was something else in her heart. Forgiveness from Mary. And the promise that soon, very soon, she could play with pie-crust in the pantry.

Miss Gilmore didn't laugh as she told me this story. Perhaps the memory of her delightful childhood was upon her. There was the time she called on the wife of a Methodist preacher who lived next door and sniffed the air like a young colt. "I'll bet that sage-dressing doesn't taste as good as it smells," said she, significantly, to Mrs. Tupper. There was the time she first watched Grandmother Gilmore pickling peaches and preserving quinces. . . . There was the time Grandmother Sprague taught her, patiently, to make pie-crust. . . . There was the Sunday she slid down the nearby gully, not once but many times, as the only appropriate climax to rice pudding at a friend's house. There was the time she asserted her small ego by calmly sitting down, in the midst of a Maypole dance, to lace up the ribbons of her ballet slippers. . . . There were the innumerable times she tried to run away to Troy—Troy, New York.

"And all through your childhood you were interested in food?" I asked Miss Gilmore.

"Always! I even kept a scrap-book for special recipes. I had, as a mere child, a great ambition to serve a meal beautifully."

Most children love their mother's kitchen, but if they cook anything, it is to boil a watery fudge which declines to harden. Not so Marion Gilmore. Her first culinary achievement was pop-overs which popped! So light they were, so golden-brown, so just right, that presently the little girl was parading around the neighborhood demonstrating pop-overs.

Miss Gilmore must have read the surprise on my face.

"It isn't so amazing," she declared, in her matter-of-fact manner. "It was merely that my mother let me share in the work of our home and taught me how to do it well. She was most particular about the house. Everything had to be thus and so, immaculate."

I looked at the shining pans. She was her mother's daughter. . . .

"So," said I, "even then you wanted to grow up and be a dietitian?"

"No," she replied slowly. "Music appealed to me more. I remember listening to Nellie, my little chum, play *The Doll's Dream* and wishing, passionately, that I could play it. I asked my father to buy me a piano. And he did. Whereupon I learned, proudly, to play. Later, I began to sing. At that time to become a singer was my great ambition. After I was graduated from high school, I studied music at the New England Conservatory and later under Madame Munger. Then my father had financial reverses, and well, you know the rest."

Yes, I knew the rest. But, strangely, I couldn't bring myself to be sorry. The world had lost a singer and gained a dietitian. Was that a matter for sorrow?

From music to domestic science was a considerable wrench. Marion Gilmore went to Simmons College in Boston for some special subjects. Then she completed a course at Miss Farmer's School of Cookery in the same city and she became director of domestic science at the Malden high school. One position led to another. She was dietitian in the St. Luke's hospital in Chicago. She was manager of the Swift Industrial Cafeteria in Omaha. She managed the tea room in the Sheridan-Plaza Hotel in Chicago. A friend then persuaded her to return to hospital work, and for

three years she was buyer and dietitian at the
Chicago Henrotian Hospital. And now she is
back in the "hotel game," this time in the Pennsylvania Hotel of New York City.

"Which do you like better," I asked, "the hospital field or the commercial field?" I knew that
dietetics are divided roughly, into two classes:
dietetics for sick people and dietetics for well
people.

She didn't hesitate for the fraction of an instant. "The commercial," she said. "To me, hospitals are tiresome because of the routine,
although I have friends who prefer hospital work
to any other."

She didn't look as if she had ever, from the
time she was born, found anything tiresome,
anything depressing. There was an open-air quality about the woman. For the moment, I got no
hint of pop-overs or *The Doll's Dream* or a dietitian's office. She looked like green hills and a long
stride. Was her bobbed hair responsible for the
illusion, or her heather-colored tweed suit, or her
substantial oxfords?

"What, exactly, are your duties here at the
Pennsylvania?" I asked.

"I supervise the serving of five meals a day to
twenty-three hundred employees. Since hotel
guests order *à la carte,* there is no dietary kitchen
for the main guests' dining room, although it is
true a few resort hotels do maintain such a

kitchen. I have my own kitchen, my own crew. I serve three full-sized meals a day, a nine-in-the-evening lunch, and a midnight supper for the night cleaners. By giving them a good square meal, I manage to keep them well and happy and eager to coöperate.

"I plan the menus for all these meals. I order the supplies. I supervise the preparing and serving of the food. I employ the staff. And see that adequate records are kept. And I enjoy it all," she said. "I enjoy it because of what I do. And I enjoy it because I realize that every day of my experience is giving me something of value in the field of dietetics. Not a year goes by but I have opportunity to enter this or that other interesting position. Yet I am distinctly not a genius in this work. It is merely that the demand for trained and experienced dietitians exceeds the supply.

"More and more people are coming to realize the importance of right food. For every dietitian who goes out from her training course, I would say that six are in demand. Hospitals need them, colleges, schools, cafeterias, hotels, tea rooms, social centers, medical centers, all kinds of institutions. Summer camps need them. High schools need them as teachers in the domestic science classes.

"It is a promising field for the girl who enjoys going into the kitchen, who doesn't mind being cook at house parties or on camp trips, with the important consideration, I would say, that of securing good training. If a girl can afford it, I would recommend that she plan, to attend college, taking her courses in home economics as part of her college education. The most important and interesting positions in the field of dietetics are increasingly being filled by young women who are college graduates.

"But a college degree is not necessary. A two-year intensive course in dietetics will fit a girl to occupy a good position in this field. And if she later finds that more training is desirable, she can arrange to take it. State universities and colleges offer this training. And there are special schools of home economics. The girl who is interested should inquire about them."

"But what if a girl cannot afford any training?" I asked.

"It is the same in this field as in many others," replied Miss Gilmore. "It is possible to learn by experience. Many young women who have not had special dietetic training have successfully managed tea rooms or lunch rooms. And some have had their own enterprises and have made them a financial success.

"I could take you to a woman, not far from here, who has never studied in any such course, yet who is in charge of a large restaurant. She has worked in restaurants for many years and during that time has gained a valuable knowledge of what the general public likes to eat, away from home. Her restaurant is especially popular with men. It is thronged with them during the lunch period."

"And I know a woman who was always a splendid housekeeper," I added. "She and her husband bought a little place near a large girls' camp. One summer she decided to open a tea room, specializing in chicken and waffles. It has been a great success. And when I talked with her about it not long ago, she said that planning and cooking her own meals at home and also the innumerable church suppers of which she used to be chairman gave her just the experience she needed for her tea room."

"Exactly," said Miss Gilmore. "If, however, a girl wishes to get into such special work as hospital dietetics, I would say that training is essential. There are certain phases of scientific feeding which only the scientist is qualified to teach. The results of the latest research work along nutritional lines are given in the class room. A study is made of those special diets needed to remedy bad bodily conditions. Courses in chemistry of foods are included in the curriculum.

"In short, I would say that if a young woman is interested in this field and has opportunity to take training in it, she should consider carefully before she chooses the longer road of learning by experience. Training first, experience afterward is what I believe to be wisest in the end.

"Another advantage which I would mention in connection with the field of dietetics is the variety of openings. A girl is not limited in her choice. She can choose the surroundings that most appeal to her in almost any part of the country, for people eat everywhere! She will perhaps become an assistant in the dietetic work of a large organization. Or she may be put in charge of it in a smaller enterprise. If she proves that she has executive ability and can direct the work of others, as well as accomplish her own dietetic work effectively, she will almost certainly be able to step into a more important administrative position.

"There are draw-backs, of course. Most dietitians have to stand constantly on their feet. Often the hours are long. There are crises when the very sight of food is distasteful. And there are the inevitable difficulties that daily arise in any work that involves numbers of people. But to me the thing-in-itself is sufficiently interesting to carry me over these difficulties. And I believe it will be for any girl who finds this work decidedly to her taste.

"But even this is not all. I like to think of what

dietitians everywhere are doing for the health of this country. The importance of a wholesome diet cannot be underestimated. Some dietitians are engaged in directly educating people what to eat. But I believe that all of us are having a very real share in this important health education. Wherever an excellently balanced and well-cooked meal is served, I am certain that not only are those served benefiting by it when they eat it; I believe that they carry away with them a memory of it which will help to guide them in future choices of food. I know that much of what I learned at home was not consciously taught me by my mother. I absorbed it simply by being where certain things were done well. It is the same way with well chosen food."

We were standing now in the pastry room of the hotel guests' dining room, among the devil's food cake stuffed with thick marshmallow, little tea cakes, French pastry, hazel-nut wafers, and crusty peach pies. What a fabulous setting for the little girl, grown tall, who had a double dream: to play the piano and to concoct a cocoa-nut cake. Half the dream, at least, has come true. Did her father, when he told Marion, laughingly, that she would have to "move the piano into the kitchen or the stove into the parlor," ever suspect that Marion would some day, figuratively, move the piano into the kitchen? For Mr. Statler's gigantic kitchen is, today, her business; music is her recreation.

"Won't you have a cake?" said Miss Gilmore in her hostess voice, not her executive voice.

"Thanks," said I, and sank my unreluctant teeth into a rich chocolate eclair.

PEGGY HOYT

A girl who
had a knack
with clothes

PEGGY HOYT

IT was fitting that I should talk to Peggy
Hoyt in the presence of strawberries and
tulips. Especially when the regal red of the strawberries matched both the gown she wore and the
mouth into which the strawberries disappeared so
daintily. Especially when the tulips were February tulips, and lavender-flowered, green-leafed,
black-seeded. The green blended with the wall
just behind it. The lavender, dyed a delicate blue
at center, added just the right touch of——

"Tenderness," said Peggy Hoyt. "To me,
always, mauve and lavender say tenderness."

She spoke simply, unaffectedly. This was no
color dictum, no professional statement. It was
as if a child had looked upon color, and delighted.
No wonder Aubrey Eads, her very adequate husband, calls her on occasion "my child." After all,

167

didn't the Earl of Surrey in the sixteenth century say and with insight, that most people "are child-like in the best things, till they be cradled in their grave"?

Yet this particular "child" is the main prop of Peggy Hoyt, Incorporated. She it is who creates the hats and cloaks and gowns which have made her famous, who arbitrates among her customers and her employees with a monumental tact, who has forced the great French dressmakers to murmur "genius." With her unerring fashion-sense, she is able to anticipate almost every style. Very often she innovates. She was the first, for instance, since Madame Pompadour, to imitate the ancient turban of the Rajahs with the modern draped crown; the first to trim hats with embroidery; the first to use the rhinestone ornaments which were the "rage" in 1925.

The story of these rhinestone ornaments illustrates, very well, one of the Peggy Hoyt methods of designing. Method, here, is half accident. In doing the original costumes for *The Merry Widow*, she fastened little rhinestone wings on the heels of the dancing slippers. But, owing to their interference with stepping, they were straightway discarded. A week or so later, while experimenting with the black satin of a turban of a society woman who is more beautiful in a black-and-white way than any other society woman is supposed to be, Peggy Hoyt stuck two of the rhinestone wings into her hat. Charming! The very cap of Mercury. . . . And the style was set.

But she has other more definitely planned methods of creation. Sometimes Peggy Hoyt starts with a color combination, sometimes with a textile combination, sometimes with a novel decoration, sometimes with a re-adaptation of an age-old style. This re-adaptation of historical costumes is perhaps the richest source of present-day fashions. From time to time the Empire influence is in the ascendancy, or the Greek, or the Russian peasant, or the early Egyptian. Often two periods are picturesquely combined. But more often, I think, Peggy Hoyt gets an idea seemingly out of the blue void and waits for the inspiration—for it is an inspiration—which will incorporate it, enchantingly, into an original costume.

"Suppose, for instance," she confided over her strawberries, "that I wanted to use these tulips in a gown. At first it might appear impossible. Tulips! And then, suddenly, a means of getting their color or their shape would present itself. Perhaps they would turn out to be a bold tulip-border around the bottom of a dress and up the skirt."

I looked at the tulips in question. Without being at all sentimental, I saw Peggy Hoyt as a flower. The color of tulips, I mused, but not these

tulips. . . . They were such sturdy little fellows.
. . . What flower, then? Not snapdragons,
though they were mighty near it. . . . Wild
Columbine! That was it! They are a deeper lavender, more delicate on their stems, and very gay
in the wind. Yes—wild columbine!

But I was wandering from the practical. Designing is a serious profession with hazards,
handicaps, spurs, and set-backs. It requires a
great talent for clothes and, if the designer runs
her own shop, a talent for dealing with people.
Women are prone to be inordinately fussy when
it comes to purchasing their wardrobe. They
want this concession; they want that price; they
demand special consideration; they declare that
the gown was not delivered as promised; they
fume about the alterations; they long, so, to be
flattered.

"But we won't flatter them," said Mr. Eads,
who is the business partner of his wife, "even
though we realize that flattery will make a woman
buy anything. A frock is, or it is not, becoming.
A hat is, or it is not, *chic*."

Peggy's creations are *chic*. It is this essential
smartness upon which the high reputation of
her establishment rests. Women are proud to be
seen sitting in her salon.

Peggy Hoyt was born (in Saginaw, Michigan)
with a feeling for fashion. She used to sit up in
her high-chair and draw circles with tails attached

and insist upon calling these tad-poles "ladies." Later, as a child in New York, she made exquisite eight-inch paper dolls which were the envy of every little girl in the neighborhood. She put hats on them, and dresses, and coats that weren't ordinary coats. At twelve, ambitious to be a sketcher, she drew little place-cards which caused at least one man to say: "Lovely! Go to it, Peggy!"

An only child, she was sent to a finishing school in New Jersey, and rebelled. Pratt Institute in Brooklyn, where she studied design after her father's death, was more to her liking. Even then, in spite of her mother's decision that she, and not her daughter, should go into the commercial world, Peggy plotted to go into business. She came home one day to announce, "I've gone into millinery."

Peggy was indispensable in that millinery shop. She had a decided knack with hats. When the proprietor brought in a shipment of French hats, she it was who tried them on at just the correct angle. In the actual making of millinery, she was adroit. Both her fingers and her imagination could travel fast.

At the end of a year's apprenticeship, she went into the hat business for herself. Everyone said she was a little mad. But they admired her pluck. Her boarding school friends were ardent customers and ardent press-agents. They, in turn, buttonholed their friends with a, "You've got to buy a hat from Peggy!" But the real reason for the success of Peggy Hoyt's shop near Forty-second Street on the Avenue was the brave originality, the sheer beauty, of her hat models.

When Forty-second Street became hopelessly congested, Peggy moved her shop to the old Philip Rhinelander house on Fifty-Fifth. There is a delicacy about the finishing there, a dignity about the marble staircase, which reflects admirably the spirit of the woman. She started at her new place of business to make dresses which were as stunning as her hats. There was youth in their lines, youth in their colors. It is as if Peggy Hoyt could repeat, in her frocks, that motto on King Edward's sundial which long ago she took as her own:

"Let others tell of rains and showers,
"I only record the sunny hours."

Something of that joyous spirit was in the costume she wore the first day I saw her—a rich red leather coat relieved with beige fur, a red close-draped hat, and a red purse touched, audaciously, with purple. "The best dressed woman?" Yes, in the artist's sense.

"Color," said Miss Hoyt. "So much can be expressed through it. Once, perhaps because I was dressed in red as a child, or because red was associated in my mind with wickedness, I had a prejudice against all reds. The Moscow Art Theater converted me. Now I use red without hesitation."

"You love color," I said. "Have you any other special enthusiasms in clothes?"

She nodded. "Soft fronts," said she. "Women love them, you know. A bit of chiffon or lace at the throat."

"Anything else?" I asked.

"Long lines. They seem to me so much more artistic than short, choppy lines."

"Artistic!" She approaches her medium of expression from the same angle that artists in paint, or clay, or words, approach their medium. Color, contour, harmony, contrast. . . . Designing, then, at its best, is an art, in that the designer takes known materials, puts them together in a new and heretofore unknown way, and produces a thing of beauty.

Shall the girl who thinks that she would like to become a designer go about it as Peggy Hoyt did? Yes—even though there are not many with her superlative gift.

"If you have a way with clothes," says Peggy Hoyt, "if you enjoy the very touch of the needle, if you revel in yards of new material, you may know that you at least have aptitude for the work."

But what comes next?

"That depends," continues Peggy Hoyt. "A

course in an excellent school of design will help
you. There are more such schools today than there
were when I started out, although my alma
mater still ranks high. And there are few large
cities without at least elementary courses in design."

Girls of all degrees of education are admitted
to these schools of design. You need not have a
college degree to enter them. High school and
grammar school graduates are equally welcome
provided they have aptitude for this work and a
thorough knowledge of dressmaking. This knowledge of dressmaking may be gained through practical experience anywhere—at home, in a workshop, or in a dressmaking course such as is offered
in many schools.

Any excellent course in dress design is shaped
to meet the practical needs of the professional
designer. A designer must be able to plan a gar-
ment in detail, to sketch a model, drape and cut
the material and, in case of necessity, do the
actual sewing. Courses in design teach these steps,
enabling the student to work with all kinds of
materials. Students also study the costumes of
other days, making original designs adapted from
the earlier styles. They visit museums and art
galleries. They attend fashion shows where they
see the most recent creations of world-famous
designers. In short, they study clothes wherever
and whenever they are displayed. They turn to

paintings and beautiful objects for inspiration in the motifs of their designs. And as long as they continue in this field they will study clothes and beautiful things in this way.

"But whether the shop work comes before or afterward or 'with' a course in design," says Peggy Hoyt, "it must come sometime. No girl who is serious in her wish to progress as a designer can dispense with it. She must serve her apprenticeship there."

And so the choice of the shop becomes highly important. It will inevitably be a workshop in a large city, for that is where opportunities for designers are to be found. If you can enter one that is known for the originality and craftsmanship of its creations, you are fortunate. Here, no matter how humble or routine the tasks which are given you to perform, you will see gowns and other garments in all stages of construction. You will see how the work is planned and organized. You will be able to watch the head designers who preside over the various work tables, as they go about the details of their tasks. You will see them combine colors, adapt a popular style in various ways. Often these heads are given cost limits beyond which they may not go. The apprentice becomes acquainted with the economies which keep a design within those cost limits yet do not sacrifice effectiveness. The more capable the head worker under whom a girl works, the more valuable her workshop experience will be to her.

And if your work is skillfully executed, if in the opportunities which are given you for making decisions you show instinctive good taste, you are taking the first steps toward becoming a head designer, in charge of a table, as the group of girls who carry out designs is called.

Many girls in workshops today have a story not unlike that of Peggy Hoyt, even though they may not have her ability. Some are girls who, in their small home towns, enjoyed sewing and became local dressmakers, later going to a city for their course in design and workshop experience. Not all have become head designers. Not all will ever become head designers. In any field, there are always fewer heads than workers. But they have found work to their taste.

Designing is not, however, a field without difficulties. A girl must work in a room where the noise of whirring machines is sometimes unbearable, yet she must bear it. There are rush seasons, because women buy most of their clothes during certain limited times of the year and the clothes must be ready for them to buy. During these rush seasons, a girl must work feverishly, often overtime. If mistakes are made, there is sometimes little sympathy from the head of the workroom, who is herself rushed and tired. Much depends upon the person under whom a girl serves her apprenticeship. She may be a sympathetic woman, interested in helping a beginner and giving her the benefit of her own experience. Or she may be a woman jealous of any real ability in her assistants. Every beginner is apt to meet injustice and jealousy.

For those who, like Peggy Hoyt, combine craftsmanship and an instinctive feeling for style with a desire to sell the clothes that are made, there is the possibility of later opening a shop of their own. Peggy Hoyt is an able business woman. Without becoming the driver into which many professional women degenerate, she is never betrayed by her gentleness into bad business. It is her belief that a woman, whether she has a vocation or an avocation, should be, like the French, "of the salon." Business is not incompatible with femininity, she declares. And to demonstrate this, she remains the delicate thing which is, inimitably, Peggy Hoyt.

"Eventually," said someone—I forget whether it was Peggy Hoyt or Aubrey Eads—"New York will be a Mecca of fashions. Americans have an instinctive good taste in the clothes they wear. Our designers are original. They are daring. Yes, before many years have passed, New York will be a Mecca of fashions."

Good news, surely, for the girl who is interested in design.

JEAN NORRIS

*A girl who courageously
entered a field
men said belonged to them*

JEAN NORRIS

JEAN had been rude to her teacher. Together with the other eleven-year-olds in her class, she had flounced her skirt, and flounced her tongue, and flounced her small and rebellious spirit. The proud something in Jean Hortense Giles-Noonan which caused her schoolmates to change Hortense to "Horty," and "Horty" to "Haughty," was now running rampage. And she wasn't sorry. On the contrary. After school she boasted about it to her chum, boasted so loudly that her father overheard.

"Jean," said her father, when the chum had departed, "were you guilty of such rudeness?"

"Yes, Father." She was rather pleased over her ability to vent her imperiousness upon a grown school-teacher.

Major Giles-Noonan thereupon turned into a thunder-cloud. "Then tomorrow you will publicly beg your teacher's pardon. No—don't say you can't. It will be hard, I know. But you were certainly in the wrong, and you must learn to acknowledge when you are in the wrong. If you stand up in front of everyone tomorrow and say: 'I'm sorry,' it will help you, Jean, all your life."

The girl was aghast. She knew her father was right. But she couldn't stand up in front of her fellow offenders and admit her guilt. She couldn't. She couldn't!

"If you are my child," said the father whom she loved, "you will."

The next day, just before dismissal, one member of the class was suffering untold agony. She couldn't do it. . . . What would her father say? . . . All in a flash, imperious little Jean was on her feet.

"Miss Jones," she cried, "my father says I was rude to you yesterday and I know I was. He says I must apologize. I do apologize—I do!"

The eyes of the teacher popped. The eyes of Jean's fellow-offenders popped. But Jean wasn't through. Having become virtuous within the last five minutes, she now became a fiery crusader.

"I was rude, but so were you," she shrilled at a small friend—"And you, and you, and you!" Her accusing finger went around the room.

One by one they apologized; one by one they regained their righteousness.

Judge Jean Norris, the only woman judge in the State of New York, smiled as she told me this story of her childhood.

"The incident had a permanent influence upon my life," she concluded. "Since the afternoon of my peculiar apology, I have never found it difficult to admit my mistakes. And that, incidentally, is a requirement for every lawyer and for every magistrate."

She spoke like what she is—a judge. Her voice was clear and calm; her presence, dignified.

A half-hour before I had been in the court room when the deep voice of one of the court attendants boomed out, "All stand. The Judge is entering the Court."

I had stood with the rest and had seen her enter, her head with its short dark wavy hair erect above the simplicity of the rolling white collar, which relieved the voluminous black robe. And I had heard her try the case of Camilla Benuto. Camilla, a dark-eyed, dark-haired young Italian girl of sixteen, weeping bitterly before the baleful eyes of her mother and the hard disdain of her older brother.

"I'm guilty. I'm guilty," Camilla had sobbed before the judge could speak. "I'm guilty. I'm guilty," she cried, piteously.

The mother could not speak English nor did she understand it. An interpreter, in Italian, conveyed Judge Norris' questions.

What had Camilla done?

She was a bad, bad girl. She stayed out nights. She went out with bad people. She was a bad, bad girl. Emphasizing her words with angry jerkings of her shawled head, Camilla's mother demanded, through the interpreter, "Put her away. I don't want her."

The judge leaned forward. "You say she has stayed out late at night. How often?" she asked in the clear, calm voice.

The mother gesticulated. The interpreter spoke. "Twice, your honor."

"Only twice—in her whole life?"

"Yes, your honor," the interpreter said, from out the flow of angry Italian.

"And where did Camilla go on those nights?"

"Once to the movies, your honor. And once to a dance at her church."

"How late did she stay out the night she went to the motion pictures?"

"Nine, your honor."

"How late was it the night she went to the church dance?"

"Ten-thirty, your honor."

"With whom did she go to the motion pictures?"

"With a girl friend from her church, your honor."

"With whom did she go to the church dance?"

"With the same friend, your honor."

"Who walked home with her?"

"The same friend, your honor."

"Anyone else?"

"No, your honor."

"And what did you do when Camilla came home late on those nights?" the judge asked of Camilla's mother.

A flood of Italian inundated the court room. The mother burst into imprecations. The brother stepped up. "I beat her good," he declared. Camilla sobbed pitifully. And the interpreter, restoring order, gave back the official reply, "Her brother beat her both times, your honor."

The judge turned to Camilla. Her eyes were very kind and there was gentle pity in her voice. "Tell me, Camilla," she said. "Do you work?"

"Yes, ma'am," replied Camilla between choking sobs, her eyes on the wooden rail before her.

"Where, Camilla?"

"To the factory."

"How much do you earn there, dear?"

There was friendliness in her honor's voice. And Camilla, feeling it, raised her head. "I get fifteen dollars a week."

"And what do you do with it?"

"I give all of it to my mother."

"How much does she give you?"

"Ten cents for my carfare and twenty-five cents for my lunch every day."

"Do you ever get any more of it to spend, Camilla?"

Camilla shook her head, the sobs rising again.

Once more the judge turned to Camilla's angry mother.

"What does Camilla do when she comes home at night?"

"She helps me with the dishes and the wash," replied the woman, through the interpreter.

"And what does she do when that is finished?"

"She goes to bed."

It was a tragic little scene, there before the judge—Camilla, the young girl, sobbing, "I'm guilty. I'm guilty." over and over, the gentleness of her bearing belying the harsh protestations of her vindictive mother and unsympathetic brother that she was a "bad girl."

Again it was toward the mother and the brother that Judge Norris directed her remarks. "Camilla is not a bad girl," she said. "Camilla is a very good girl. She gives you all her money. She has stayed out only two nights in her whole life—and then she was with her friends. Camilla is sixteen. She must have some good times. Every girl Camilla's age needs good times."

The woman was obdurate. The black-shawled head continued to jerk violently. "No. No. She is a bad, bad girl. She cannot come back. I don't want her. Put her away."

Patiently the judge persisted, earnestly trying to win from the mother some expression of love for her daughter, some flicker of understanding of a girl's need for play. But to the interpreter's words, the only reply was violent head-shakings. And the brother, joining in, added his harsh, "She's a bad girl. Put her away."

Before their hardness, the gentle, velvet-eyed Camilla shrank against the wooden railing.

At length the judge passed sentence. "The Court rules that Camilla Benuto is not guilty. She is not a bad girl. I cannot send her to a home." And once more she tried to persuade the mother to take Camilla back. Her patient effort was without avail.

It is cruel to be told you are not wanted in your own home. Camilla's head went down upon her hands. "Don't cry, dear," said the judge. "Go with this man into that room over there and I will take care of you."

The mother and the brother walked away. Camilla vanished through a doorway, led by a kind court attendant. At a gesture from the judge, another attendant came to my side. "Her honor will now call a worker from Camilla's church," he explained. "And the worker will take care of her until we can find some place for the girl to live."

"Will the judge see that she finds a place to live?" I whispered.

The court attendant smiled and nodded. "Oh, yes," he said.

It was true. Months later, seeing the judge, I asked her what had happened to Camilla.

"That poor, dear child!" said the judge. "We searched until we at last found an Italian family who were genuinely interested in having her live with them. There was a girl the same age as Camilla and the mother was an understanding soul who knew that a girl must have some fun as well as work. Camilla is still with them and she is happy there. But what do you think she does every week? She sends home to her mother part of what she earns."

Part of her earnings to her mother—harsh, stern, unrelenting.

"Yes," said the judge, sensing my thought. "Camilla and I are both hoping she will change."

Judge Jean Norris—the first woman judge in the State of New York, sitting in a court-room crowded with spectators, newspaper reporters, court attendants, lawyers, defendants and complainants—mostly men. A woman adequate to the situation, with not a man-lawyer, not a man-witness, not a man-prisoner questioning her authority nor intimating by word or gesture that they respected her less because of her womanhood.

Justice, the judge told me that morning in

her office, is the quality which, above all else,
she covets. To be just—that is her great aspira-
tion. To assemble the facts of a case, to weigh
them carefully, and to render a judgment which
is impersonal and *right*. To be just—and to understand. A woman bringing to the court-room
not only a keen knowledge of law, not only a rare
dignity, but a sympathy and an understanding
which make of her court rulings something more
than a matter of law alone. It was this understanding which was so quick to recognize Camilla
Benuto's need for play. It was this understanding
which gave her patience for the mother so gripped
by harshness and blindness, which made her willing to exhaust every resource of persuasion in an
effort to bring that mother closer to her young
daughter.

I wondered at her poise. For Jean Hortense
Giles-Noonan Norris wasn't always a judge on
the bench. She grew up as many girls grow up,
dreaming of travel and far adventure. But even
though her ancestors had been English barristers
for generations, with a strain of Irish and a strain
of Norman French, it didn't occur to Jean that
she could be a lawyer. A circus-rider, perhaps,
because she adored riding, and a circus-rider can
straddle a horse and jump through a hoop. For
a long time, she inclined to circus-riding. Later,
she shifted her allegiance from circus-rider to
surgeon.

"I'm going to study medicine," she announced to her family.

A girl—a surgeon, with knives! Unthinkable! And her horrified family set out, systematically, to discourage her latest youthful ambition.

As a matter of record, Jean embarked upon neither of these careers. When she was twenty years old, she married and settled down to a life of domesticity. But in less than two years her husband died. It was then, as a widow and at the age of twenty-two, that she decided to become a lawyer. Bravely she undertook the long course which she must pass before taking the state bar examinations: college work and three years of legal training. Two degrees from New York University and several courses in sociology at Fordham University primed her for the bar. A year later she was established in her own law office on William Street.

But the career of the girl who was nicknamed "Haughty" was more hazardous than it appears on paper. Few women, even today, are lawyers. But back in 1909, they were scarce as bluebirds in winter. When Mrs. Jean Norris took notes in law class, more than one professor looked at her dubiously. When she was ready to hang out her "shingle," landlords eyed her askance and put her off upon being informed that she wanted to rent an office. When, as an attorney, she argued a case in court, the opposing side did not always

take her seriously—to their grief. It was a fight
against odds, and she won.

For ten years she practiced law. Many a night,
while she was collecting a clientele, she worked
far into the black hours, briefing, drawing up
contracts, mulling over an affidavit. She became
widely known as a competent lawyer. Frequently
a Big Man commented on her fair-mindedness,
or a newspaper named her as an important factor
in a new legislation, or a politician praised the
work she was accomplishing with Judge Olvany
in the Tenth Assembly District as his co-leader.
She was elected president of the National Association for Women Lawyers and president of the
New York State Federation of Business and
Professional Women's Clubs. Fear and respect
—she could elicit both!

In October, 1919, she was appointed to the
magistrate's bench in New York City. She took
her seat with the dignity which characterized her
"Yes, Father," on that memorable day when
he said, "Jean Noonan, were you guilty of such
rudeness?"

For seven years she has rotated between all the
magistrates' courts in the counties of New York
and the Bronx. For seven years she has faced
the accused with level eyes, and delivered sentence. Her work, she tells me, is fascinating. Which
only proves that "what's food to one man is poison
to another." How many women could sit on a

bench all day, every day of the year, Sundays
and holidays included—and call it fascinating?
But only one woman in many is born with the
analytical brain of Jean Norris.

"Do you think," I asked her honor (how odd
the feminine sounds!) "that there are attributes
peculiar to girls which especially fit them for
law?"

"As in everything else," said Judge Norris,
"it depends upon the girl herself. There are men
who make good lawyers and women who make
good lawyers. Sex doesn't greatly matter."

"But girls *do* make good lawyers?"

"Girls in general? No. Individual girls and
individual men? Yes. It depends upon the person.
The girl who is interested in law must have a
clear mind, an ability to grasp facts and to see
the significance of facts, an ability to grasp the
law, itself, if she would be a lawyer. And she
must set herself to secure her training in a recognized law school. In law school, some young
women who have thought they wished to become
lawyers drop out. Their class work shows them
that they are unsuited for it. Other young women
discover through their study and their first experiences in the law that, despite the difficulties,
they enjoy it. Everything depends upon the girl
herself."

"Is the number of women lawyers increasing?"
I asked.

"Every year," replied Judge Norris. "Just as the number of women doctors is increasing. In law, as well as in medicine, the long training which is necessary and the time one must spend in getting experience and in gaining a clientele in order to be self-supporting, make both fields difficult to enter. The determination of anyone entering the law is tested hundreds of times— of anyone, man or woman, but especially woman. Yet those of us who love the law hold on.

"And one often comes upon women lawyers in unexpected places. Why in the court of Batavia, Java, when I went around the world, I discovered a native woman attorney—a little, dark-skinned thing, educated in Holland, I believe. You see," Judge Norris went on to explain, "we judges do have occasional weeks off duty. Before the trip which I just mentioned, I let mine accumulate to eighteen weeks. And when I started off, Judge McAdoo asked me to investigate the courts of the Orient. Accordingly, I sat beside the three judges in the native court of Cairo, Egypt; in the courts of Rangoon, Burma; Bombay and Calcutta, India; in Singapore, in Shanghai, China, and Tokyo, Japan.

"It was a fascinating experience. I have always had a hankering for strange seaports. As a little girl, the very sound of Canton was an enchantment to me. I remember we had a Chinese laundryman who was devoted to our family. At

Christmas time, he brought us gifts—once, a
queer-colored cat's eye for me. The birthplace of
that marvelous Chinaman was Canton, China. No
wonder it was glamorous!" A little girl destined
to sit behind an impressive rail and say coolly to
the court scribe, "Strike that out;" "Motion
granted;" or, "The Court finds the defendant
guilty."

I thought of all the women in the world whom
convention and prejudice have kept from the
great professions. "Women can't do this."
"Women can't do that." And I was glad that
Judge Norris is among those who have had the
courage to hold on in what they wished to do,
glad for her and glad for the girls who wish to
follow her in the law.

There are a few law schools that still do not
admit young women—but there are law schools
that do and the girl who is interested can find
out which ones they are by inquiring. And one
by one, the number of these law schools which
do admit women is becoming greater. So the girl
who is attracted to this field can today secure the
necessary training, although she must be ready
for several years of it, as Judge Norris said. Any
girl who is interested can readily ascertain the
requirements for entrance into these law schools
as well as the requirements for taking the bar
examinations in her own state.

Once having secured her training, are things

as difficult for the girl of today as they were for
Judge Norris? Yes, in many ways. Prejudice
against women lawyers still exists in some communities. People will not consult them. There
are still law offices which will not consider giving
an opening to a young woman, whereas they will
gladly make room for a young man who has been
a member of the same law class as she. Yet just
as the number of law schools which a girl may
attend is increasing, so the opportunities to enter
law offices for apprenticeship are multiplying
for her. The very fact that there has been a Judge
Norris as well as many other able practising
women lawyers and a few women judges in other
cities is constantly widening this field.

It is so, too, in other professional fields which
have long been claimed by men as exclusively
their own, such as medicine and architecture. Like
law requiring several years of special training,
like law placing obstacles in the path of even the
most determined, but like law in having had
pioneer women who have persevered, winning for
themselves the right to do the work which they
preferred, giving to others the gift of wider
opportunity.

"We are ready, your honor." It was time for
court to re-convene.

CLARA SIPPRELL

*A girl whose brother
was a photographer
and who liked to take pictures*

CLARA SIPPRELL

WHETHER the roads were gold with autumn, or white with winter, or green with early spring, Clara Sipprell loved to walk down them and dream. Why she loved them is uncertain. Because the roads were countless years old and Clara was fourteen? Because she wanted to be alone? Or because the ever-shifting light did miraculous things with the orchards and the wire fence and the acres of barley? Clara Sipprell blames the walking and the dreaming on the light.

I see her, vividly, on the roads. Her legs are long, her pigtail is long, and her dreams are long —long. It is not difficult to imagine her eager figure, as solitary as a lark on a fence-post. It is not difficult, even though I first saw Clara Sipprell when she was nearer forty than fourteen, and when the roads around Buffalo had been exchanged for a New York studio. I cannot decide whether I like the girl better, or the woman. She wore, that day I saw her in her studio, a black mandarin coat over a sea-green gown that

matched, in color, her sea-green beads, and
matched, in spirit, the high comb which topped
the red-brown swirl of her hair. Her face was
fine and proud and sensitive, as she told me of
her childhood which preceded her work as a
photographer. She was obviously an artist.

"I just grew like Topsy," she admitted in her
low-pitched voice. "My brother was a boy and
I was a boy—together. I didn't care much for
school. I didn't care much for anything on earth
except walking on the roads around Buffalo, and
dreaming. Those hours alone were the high-points
in my childhood."

Clara Sipprell's mouth was whimsical, and her
voice was whimsical, and her whimsicality was
contagious.

"But you went to grammar school and to high
school?" I inquired.

"Oh, yes. But what I loved most were the roads
in the moonlight and the noonlight and the just-
before-dusk light."

"And you took pictures?"

"At that time? No, indeed. I didn't own a
kodak."

This, from Clara Sipprell, the woman who has
made photography a full-fledged art!

"You went to art school, then? Or a school of
photography?"

"No. All my early training was in my brother's
studio in Buffalo. Some people learn the prin-

ciples of light and shade and composition in a school, but I didn't."

And she told me the story.

When Clara Sipprell was nineteen years old, she left school. One morning in May she presented herself at the studio of her brother. He was then a photographer of repute in Buffalo. But he was more than that: he was a sympathetic person. He had hoped that the sister who was so dear to him would go to college. But he must have seen, on this particular morning in May, another destiny on her face. For he did not argue. He did not even question. He merely looked at her, and wondered, and said no word, and let her stay.

So she learned the business of photography from the ground up. It was exciting. Her brother bought her a kodak, and she proceeded joyously to "take" everything and everybody in Buffalo, sometimes four or five on a plate. Her mistakes were many; her enthusiasms were many. One day her brother showed her two pictures and said, "Which is good and which is bad?" She did not know. At that time she was absorbed in the mechanics of developing a picture, retouching it, printing it, finishing it, enlarging and reducing it.

Later, she studied the fine points of photography. She came to have a discriminating judgment when her brother held up two pictures and said: "Which is good and which is bad?" By then, she was the owner of a camera on a tripod and the humble partner of Frank J. Sipprell.

"I was his partner for ten years," she said, "and in all that time the smell of the dark room never failed to thrill me!"

Those were important years. There being so many opportunities in the big realm of photography, she came, often, to a fork in the road. Should she continue with her brother or should she go out into other kinds of photographic work? Should she, for instance, enter commercial photography, taking pictures to illustrate stories in magazines or newspapers? There are many such photographers, today. Or should she become a photographer connected with an advertising concern taking pictures of the latest models in dresses or furniture or what-not? There are such photographers, too, and young women among them. Such work was possible for her, had she wished it. And it would have been possible for her to enter photographic work in a museum, taking pictures of the collections; or work in a scientific research laboratory, photographing the results of some scientist's long hours in the laboratory. All of us have seen such pictures in scientific magazines. Any girl who is well-grounded in the fundamentals of photography, who has been willing to spend the hours and days and even years of time which Clara Sipprell spent in learning, can branch out into some one of these many photographic fields.

Clara Sipprell branched into none of them. She worked steadily on, learning her craftsmanship, gaining invaluable experience in the smallest details of taking pictures, laying the foundation for what she was later to do. In time, she came to see what it was she really wished to undertake.

It was not "regular" photography, although she realized that there was real opportunity for her in Buffalo, particularly if she were to develop a specialty as many young women have done in the taking of children's pictures, of homes or of gardens. But because she believed profoundly in the artistic possibilities of picture-making, because beauty was, of all things, most desirable, she decided to give her talents exclusively to portraiture and to the creative photography of landscapes and still life. Who wants *just* to photograph, she thought, when she can photograph the inside soul of a person, or a snow-shadow, or a Killarney rose in a water jug? And she decided to continue her work where the art galleries and the museums and the concerts and artists themselves would give her a new touch with beauty and the creating of beautiful things. She decided to go to New York.

"When I left Buffalo," Miss Sipprell told me, "I was known as a photographer. In New

York—! Well, I kept very quiet for five years.
I didn't hurry. Nothing good comes from hurry.
In the beginning, I had enough money saved to
finance my plan. Gradually, through my friends,
I secured enough commissions to support myself
and so to continue my experiments.

"I did portraits of as many kinds of people as
I could. My friends were more than generous in
posing for me and in obtaining opportunities for
me to make portraits of interesting people whom
they knew—of painters and business men and
musicians and writers and children. Little by
little, I began to receive requests for my work
from people whom I had never met. And little by
little, I gleaned from my many attempts and
experiments, those methods which more nearly
brought the results I was after. In time, I had
a collection of pictures which, although none was
entirely what I wished it to be, nevertheless were
good. Then I was ready for an exhibit."

Clara Sipprell paused, glancing quizzically at
the photographs upon the walls opposite and at
the large books which lay upon a nearby table.
"It takes such a short while to tell you of it," she
said, "and it was so long in the doing! There on
the wall and in these books you see the pictures
which I like best of all that I have done. You do
not see the many I rejected, which fell short. You
do not know the hours I spent, only to meet fail-

ure in the end. For there have been such pictures and such hours, many of them, and they are no less part of my work than the others."

"Tell me about your exhibits," I asked.

"Exhibits are an important part of every artist's life. To go over everything that you have done, selecting various types of pictures, stopping carefully to consider which are the best of each type, arranging them together in a large room where others may come to see them is in itself a stimulating thing to do. And the opportunity which an exhibit gives you to show your work to others is stimulating. From the comments of the visitors who come to look at your pictures, you often gain great inspiration and help. The comments, unfavorable as well as favorable, reveal your work to you in a new light. You get dozens of ideas for new experiments!

"And if those who come like what they see, there is widened demand for your work. It is enough, of course, for a real artist to have created a beautiful thing. Yet artists must live, after all. And exhibits help them to do so by bringing their work before the public.

"I have held exhibits in New York and Washington and other cities in this country. I have held them in Paris and London. And last year, when I traveled through Yugoslavia, photographing quaint landscapes and quaint people, I ended with an exhibit in Constantinople. Oh, there is so much beauty to be caught with a camera!"

She showed me, quietly, a group of her pictures. A house with the sun melted and poured over it. . . . Mrs. Coolidge. . . . Leaves and their delicate shadows. . . . Rachmaninoff, the musician. . . . An old New England farmhouse, taken in Vermont where she has her summer studio. . . . An English girl, very young and very wistful . . . An old church . . . A street in Italy . . . Cloud and wind above Dalmatian poplars . . . They moved me as a great poem moves me.

"They are as beautiful as etchings!" said I, enchanted. I meant it as a compliment. But Clara Sipprell took it otherwise.

"You mustn't compare photography with painting or with etching," she warned. "It is true that an etcher or a painter, like myself, is concerned with the witchery of light and shadow, and studies the line and mass and contour of his subject. But the methods are so different. I use no paint, no pencil. The camera, with its many limitations, is my medium. In accepting those limitations and transcending them with beauty, photography becomes a real art."

A real art. Looking at her pictures, I did not doubt what Clara Sipprell said. I was not even amazed when she added that she never enlarges a picture, now, nor reduces it, nor retouches it in any way. Neither does she use artificial light. The natural thing is the beautiful thing, she maintains, and if she sufficiently understands her subject and the light falling over it, the lens can do the rest.

"Which would you rather photograph," I asked, "people or things?"

"People!"—without hesitation. "Portraiture is much more fascinating to me than still life. I try to catch that essential something which distinguishes every person from every other person —personality, spirit—call it what you will. I call it (for lack of a better name) 'the constructive moment.'"

"But some people haven't a spark," I said.

"Everyone has a spark," she corrected. "The spirit is there, hidden, and the camera must find the right angle from which to photograph it."

"Everyone is photographable?" I cried.

"Everyone," she repeated. "But the gift for portraiture is a requirement for the work. And you cannot learn it. You are either born with it or you are not."

I wondered why, since she is so greatly interested in photographing people, she spends so much time on still life.

"To do anything well," she explained, "you must do well whatever is related to it. There are 'backgrounds' in many of my portraits and I must know how to photograph those backgrounds artistically. Besides, after photographing a lovely landscape, I come back refreshed to photograph, say, a great novelist. Portraiture, you see, is not easy. I cannot do distinctive work in it if I am tired or rushed or harried."

She looked so colorful as she sat there talking that I wondered how she could content herself in photography, with blacks and greys and whites.

"How can you?" I asked.

For a moment, she stared at the sea-green of her gown.

"Easily," she said at last. "Because I get the quality of color, the richness of color—or the lack of it—in these grays and blacks. Do you understand what I mean?"

I was not sure. But I was very sure of something else. Clara Sipprell is happy, not so much because she is successful in a wordly sense, not because she is internationally known, but because she is doing the work which, more than anything else, is *her* work. If she were still experimenting in Buffalo, she would be happy, I knew.

"You smile," I ventured, "because you found, at nineteen, the work for which you were cut out."

"Is that an accusation?" she laughed.

At this moment, a vivacious, light-haired young woman came into the room. "My partner," introduced Miss Sipprell. "When my work grew, I found it impossible to attend to all the business

details and my portraiture, as well. It has all gone
much more smoothly since I have had a partner
to attend to my schedule and all my business
arrangements.

"Just now, we are working on a series of pictures of flower arrangements which a women's
magazine is to publish. My partner has inter-
viewed the editor, planned for the delivery of the
finished photographs and come to an agreement
regarding the remuneration. Since I started with
my work years ago, appreciation of beautiful pictures has grown rapidly, and appreciation of
photography as an art. This magazine connection
is a single instance. The girl who loves to take
pictures will do well to consider the possibility
of entering photography as a profession."

Books of lovely photographs are available
for the girl who is interested in photography,
Clara Sipprell went on to tell me, as well as books
of practical ways and means. Many communities
have in them those who have taken up photography as a hobby, or photographers who are striving to do beautiful work. Such people will give
a girl many helpful suggestions. There are, too,
a few schools of photography where a girl may
secure training, although Clara Sipprell does
not regret that she came through the school of
studio experience.

Silence fell upon the room with its beautiful
pictures upon every side. Again, in my imagina-

tion, I saw the fourteen-year-old Clara Sipprell walking the roads of Buffalo, watching the morning light on maple leaves and the evening light in hedgerows, and dreaming not impossible dreams. . . .

MARGARET E. MALTBY

A girl
who always
asked "why?"

MARGARET E. MALTBY

W HEN Margaret Maltby
was still in short dresses, she always wanted to
know why. Why did water boil? Why did an eye-
dropper suck up liquid? Why did it snow?

Her parents encouraged her. They showed her
how to run simple machinery, how to drive a
nail, how to put in a screw. They never said,
"Girls shouldn't do such things. They are for
boys."

Today Margaret Maltby is a professor of
physics. Who can say whether she inherited her
scientific and mechanical turn of mind from a
father who was fond of mathematics? Her childhood predilections were, at any rate, a prophecy
of her life-long interest. How fortunate she was!
So many parents take for granted that their
daughters are unscientific. They provide no
books, no encouragement, no apparatus when a
girl asks, "Why this—why that?" With such
handicaps, it is remarkable that any girls have discovered their taste for things scientific. But high

school laboratories have helped. Bicycles have helped, and machinery to tinker with. Automobiles help, with a more intricate engine for mechanical experimentation. And radio is teaching girls, as well as boys, electricity. But Margaret Maltby had the disadvantage of being taught, in high school, no science except mathematics. When she entered college and started seriously upon her scientific studies, she was handicapped.

Today, at commencement time in Columbia University, Margaret Maltby says goodbye to young women who, in their high school days, studied an interesting variety of science courses in well-equipped laboratories such as she herself did not have; who have had college courses such as she did not have; and before whom is open an opportunity for entering many more kinds of scientific work than were available for her when she, herself, completed her graduate study.

Some of these college girls, who have studied under Miss Maltby, are going out to enter her own kind of work—teaching. They are planning to become teachers of chemistry or physics or botany or geology, in high schools or boarding schools or colleges or universities. Whatever the branch of science which most interests them, if they are qualified to teach it, an opportunity is to be found.

Some enter laboratories. And if you are a girl

who gazes bewilderedly about your own laboratory with its test tubes, if you are a girl to whom "Chemistry, required" is, in plain English, dead, you may look differently upon this laboratory research done by young scientists when you know that the laboratory may be in a hospital, where the tests made will show the doctors just what treatment some very sick patient needs. Or in a nutrition center, where thin, badly nourished children are studied and helped. Or in a public health laboratory where the tests will show whether or not the water is pure on some camp site where several hundred girls are planning to camp. And if the tests show impurities, without a doubt those girls are saved from typhoid fever or other illnesses. Or the tests may be made on certain milk, with the lives of many babies in the community at stake. When you realize this, you see why scientific work is so intensely interesting and worthwhile to so many people.

But there are still further opportunities open today in the field of science. Perhaps some of the young students who have studied with Margaret Maltby decide to enter one of the research departments conducted by our Department of Agriculture or by our state universities, in connection with their agricultural schools. At these agricultural stations, they study the soil of the surrounding region and test out methods by which that soil may be made more productive. Better kinds of plants are cultivated by the laboratory workers, and a knowledge of chemistry as well as of botany plays its part in their work. And the results of their work are passed on to the farmers and gardeners of that vicinity.

Those trained in psychology are finding new and fascinating work in positions in connection with schools, where children who are having difficulty in getting along with others are studied and helped or where unusual and gifted children need special training.

You can realize what a change has taken place for the girl who is interested in science, when you know that over one thousand chemists are employed by the government at Washington, in such departments as the Bureau of Mines, the Bureau of Engraving and Printing, the Department of Agriculture—and some of these chemists are young women.

But even this is not all. One girl who took her Ph.D. at Columbia, secured a fellowship for study abroad and now works in the research laboratories of the General Electric Company at Schenectady, New York. Manufacturers of foods, metals, paints, photographic materials, rubber, soap, textiles and innumerable other products employ young women scientists, if they are capable of carrying on the research which is necessary. "How can this cheese be preserved for shipping to South America?" "How can we dye this material so that it will not fade?" "This process is too expensive. Can't we substitute for some of the ingredients, at the same time keeping the flavor?" Questions such as these are asked of the young woman research worker in manufacturing plants—and she must work out the answer in her laboratory.

Another friend of Miss Maltby took her Ph.D. at the Massachusetts Institute of Technology, won the great honor of a national research fellowship, married, and is continuing her researches in the Sterling Laboratories at Yale. Without being required to teach any classes, she is a member of the Yale faculty. Marriage has been no stumbling block to her scientific career. Month after month, she goes on studying the chemical structure of certain substances found in the human body. And she finds satisfaction in realizing that her conclusions, like all scientific conclusions, will ultimately find a practical application in human life.

Science? To be a scientist is to be an adventurous discoverer. The ways of stars, the ways of flowers, of birds, of clouds; the ways of men, of their minds and their bodies; the events of other ages, traced through rocks and rivers—science has given us these. Back of knowledge, back of truth, back of modern achievement stands the scientist in his laboratory, rejecting all half-truths, seeking the Eternal Fact.

Margaret Maltby possesses, in an eminent degree, this sternly scientific mind. Her gray dress and her gray hair, as she sat talking to me, suggested something maternal; her accurate eyes and exact phrases left no crumb of doubt that she is a scientist.

"I am constantly happy," she said, "that girls of scientific bent today have a greater opportunity than ever before both for training and for scientific work, and that the girls of tomorrow will have an even greater opportunity. I am happy that, given a good college course in the sciences, they can step out into the teaching of general scientific subjects or into other positions.

"But a girl should not overlook the fact that, if she has serious aspirations as a scientist, the more important and interesting fields of science lie ahead, open only to those who have taken still further scientific training after college. There must be graduate work leading to a doctorate of science or of philosophy. And, if possible, study abroad. If a young woman is to do genuinely distinctive work in science, a broad as well as an intensive education is the first essential.

"That is why I wish every girl who is interested in science might take all possible scientific courses while she is in high school. And that she might acquire French and German along the way, as well, if she can. For a reading knowledge of both is required for a doctor's degree, and the girl

who has accomplished this study before college—
or in college—is prepared to go on, if she later
wishes to do so.

"Then, too, by studying somewhat in various
branches of science, a girl has an early opportunity to discover her personal preferences and
she is able to make her choice more readily and
happily when the time comes for her to select
one branch of science in which she shall specialize.

"But there is no short cut in the field of science.
Thorough training is necessary."

I expressed pity for the girl who wishes to be
a scientist but who cannot afford the training.
Miss Maltby told me to temper my pity. An
education is now available, she says, for every girl
who has courage and health enough to take it
and brains enough to carry it through, whether
she wishes to specialize in science or some other
field. If she has no money for her college course,
there are scholarships which are awarded to those
who are earnest and who show real attainment in
their studies. A girl can obtain work in college
by which she may supplement what she receives
through a scholarship. Or she may borrow money,
repaying it when she has later stepped out into
a position.

Difficult? It *is* difficult, Margaret Maltby admits, to earn one's way through college—sometimes so difficult that a girl must spend more than
the usual four years doing it. And she will know

many days of utter discouragement. Courage, health, brains—all three must be called upon when a girl decides to earn her own way. But unless she possesses these, the realm of science should not be the profession of her choice.

So, too, with her graduate study, a young woman can combine it with work for which she receives payment. Or before embarking upon her after-college studies, she may go out into the scientific employment which Miss Maltby's friends among young college graduates are entering, there earning the necessary money, gaining practical experience, and returning in a year or so to her further studies, and to the possibility of being awarded a fellowship. For fellowships are awarded to graduate students. And there are the Guggenheim Fellowships, which are for the more mature scholars who are engaged in important pieces of work and who show exceptional ability.

Miss Maltby herself served a long apprenticeship. An A. B., and an A. M., from Oberlin College were only the first hurdle. Having surveyed all the sciences, she decided to specialize in physics. Her B. S. was procured at the Massachusetts Institute of Technology and her Ph.D. at the Universty of Goettingen, in Germany. At the end of an additional year in research, she became research assistant to President Kohlrausch at the .Physikalisch-Technische Reischsanstalt zu Charlottenburg. This foreign training was supplemented by a year of mathematical physics with Professor Webster at Clark University. At present she is an associate professor of physics at Barnard College, Columbia University. How faithfully she has followed the Fact!

"Another reason why girls have been slow in taking up science," went on this life-long student, "is that science required a willingness to grapple with hard and involved problems, mathematical and otherwise. No one tells a girl *what to do* if she is working upon original research in some manufacturing plant. All that the head of the plant has said is, more often than not: 'Something is wrong with this process. What is it?' And the young woman must start out into the Unknown, deciding that the trouble lies with this ingredient, or that, and devising experiments which will show her whether she is right or wrong.

"Nor does the work always consist of original experimenting. There are routine tasks to be accomplished, as well. And there are other disadvantages—long hours, sometimes of great irregularity, when an important piece of investigation is going on which cannot be interrupted even for sleep. A discovery, made when in the employ of any company, becomes automatically the property of that company. The work is confining, as all laboratory research is confining. And it requires inordinate patience, for often an

experiment of days', weeks', even years' duration
proves futile in the end and the work must be
started from the beginning once more, and in a
different way.

"In the research laboratories of our great educational institutions, without a desire for the truth
at any intellectual cost, a girl would at the end
of a few intensive months find this exacting work
very irksome."

She was right. Accuracy can be obtained by
many girls but—"What's the use?" they ask.
Others seem born inaccurate. But there are ex-
ceptions. And they are the girls to whom science
is apt to call. They are those to whom science
today offers ever-increasing opportunities, even
though the field is as yet more limited than some
others.

The years of the war were important in widening this field for young women. With so many
men away, it was necessary in many positions to
try out young women of scientific training.
People soon realized that women are as capable
as men of doing scientific work and doing it with
distinction. Manufacturers who employed young
women in their laboratories as well as at their
factory machines discovered what men in many
fields have discovered—that it is the woman herself who counts, just as it is the man himself
who counts. Not women in general, nor men in
general.

"But why," I asked Miss Maltby, "did so few women assert themselves in the first stages of science?"

"Past generations," she answered, "had women who were instinctively scientific. But where could they obtain training or encouragement to pursue their scientific careers? And it does require training. It does require encouragement! Today, this is changed. The result is that we have our women scientists."

But she hastened to point out women of the past who, despite the almost insuperable difficulties, made substantial contributions to science. Madame Curie's discovery of radium, after years of patient experiment with pitchblend, opened up an entirely new field of research in atomic structure and ushered in many important applications. Madame Curie coöperated with her husband, carrying on the experiments in his laboratory.

Caroline, the sister of Sir William Herschel, was his co-worker in astronomy. In the nineteenth century, Maria Mitchell of Vassar was the first woman to be elected to the American Academy of Arts and Science because of her distinguished work in astronomy. The Maria Mitchell Observatory is gratefully named after her. And during the recent total eclipse of the sun, this observatory's powerful glass was important in the scientific recording of that momentous event. Ellen

H. Richards won distinction as a sanitary chemist and social economist and was one of the pioneers to whom girls of today who enjoy their domestic science courses owe most. For it was she and her associates who first developed the plan to give such work in our schools.

"But, Miss Maltby," I interposed, "every girl who takes scientific training can't be a Maria Mitchell or an Ellen H. Richards—nor as able as those of your friends whose work you have described. What of the others, those who will never be able to do more than satisfactory work, in some relatively unimportant position?"

From the breadth of her experience, Margaret Maltby smiled. "Yes," she said, "of course there are such young women. But no more in science than in any other field where girls find work. The important consideration is—do they enjoy their work? Is it worthwhile? Is most of it interesting to them? *All* of it can't be to any of us, anywhere. Then—is she making fullest use of her ability? If she is, why worry about being one of those who lead the procession? It is never where you are that counts so much as——"

"As?"

"As finding satisfaction in what you are doing and doing it, to the best of your ability."

"Do you think," I said, "that women can ever be as radically original, as pioneering, as men have been in the sciences?"

"Original?" Miss Maltby repeated the word. "Of course. Why not? Wasn't Madame Curie original? Give a well-trained, imaginative woman scientist a *real opportunity* and she will be original. Up to this time, many women capable of outstandingly original work have been forced to direct their ideas and their energy to the attaining and the keeping of any kind of opening in the field of science, to winning for themselves and others the *right* to do their special kind of work. But as I have said this situation is gradually being bettered and for this reason I believe we shall have more important and more original work from our young women scientists.

"But originality requires, behind and beyond curiosity and wide and deep knowledge of the science, courage, and infinite care in detail work and constructive imagination. Imagination to see the scientific problem as a whole, to resolve it into its parts, to devise experiments which will eventually lead to the goal of solving the problem. As in the study of the structure of the atom, which is fundamental to chemistry and physics, a girl must first visualize the mechanism of the atom according to some theory, then predict its behavior under certain conditions, work out experiments to test that prediction, and finally modify the theory to fit the facts."

The facts! How at every turn, she came back to them. No scientist can talk long without be-

traying a vast reverence for things as they are,
naked and unadorned. Therein lies the truth.
And nothing less than the truth is satisfying to
these brave intellects. They repeat, with the
Dying Grammarian:

> "Let me know all! Prate not of most or least,
> "Painful or easy!"

If they renounce much, they gain much.

The "much" gained by years of study and
research in the enchanting realm of physics was
now, at this moment, on the fine and determined
face of Margaret Maltby'

BRENDA PUTNAM

*A girl who declared
at twelve she wanted to be
a sculptor*

BRENDA PUTNAM

A HUNK of clay.
A mysterious
"shape."

A rabbit.

"When I grow up,"
said twelve - year - old
Brenda Putnam, "I shall
be a sculptor."

No one laughed. No
one said, "Brenda! How
very ridiculous!" Her mother examined the little
clay rabbit which Brenda had modelled that day
in school, and complimented the absurd tail.
Her father showed his pleasure in a more con-
crete way: he bought clay and tools for his ambitious daughter and he gave her as a workshop
his own very private den. A wise father. . . .
Incidentally, he was Herbert Putnam, who was
then, and is now, librarian of Congress in Washington.

For the rabbit was, beyond a doubt, alive.
Holding it high before the modelling class,
Brenda's teacher had said so. Revolving it in his

fingers, Mr. Putnam said so. Brenda suspected it. Maybe, in a moment or two, it would leap, a brown-white blur, into the greenery, find another jack-rabbit with the same pointed ears, the same stubby tail, the same deep fur, and come back— never.

The rabbit was only a start. He was followed, in clay, by a menagerie—alley-cats, pigs, a pet dog, and a golliwock. Every little figure meant more clay "pinchings" on the floor of Brenda's 'studio," more coöperation from Mr. and Mrs. Putnam, and more determination on Brenda's part to be a sculptor.

Today her models are many. Her large, sky-lit studio is in New York City. Her determination, rewarded by prize after prize, honor after honor, is still that hard bright thing which started her on her career. Her *Sundial Figure* won the Barnett Prize at the National Academy of Design and the Widener Gold Medal at the Pennsylvania Academy of the Fine Arts. Her *Peter and the Rabbits* won the Avery Prize at the Architecture League. Her memorial to Anne Simon stands full-sized and winged, in the Rock Creek Cemetery at Washington. She executed the bust of Harriet Beecher Stowe which sits, nobly, in the Hall of Fame at New York University. At present she is at work on a bas-relief of William Dean Howells for the American Academy of Arts and Letters.

"But these so-called 'honors' are of no importance," Brenda Putnam insisted, and I had to
agree. Success in "sculping" is measured, solely,
in terms of beauty.

Beauty. . . . Beauty of form. . . . Again
and again, in her models of plastiline or clay,
Brenda Putnam achieves a physical and a
spiritual beauty. The combination, and nothing
else, makes for great sculpture. But the spiritual
significance which renders Rodin's *The Thinker*
an enduring piece of work and Brenda Putnam's
Portrait Bust of a Young Girl a praiseworthy
example of modern sculpture comes only after
long years of plugging away at the fundamentals
of this most difficult art—human anatomy, drapery, mass, proportion.

Brenda Putnam's apprenticeship was not short
and it was not easy. "Five expensive years," she
said, with a shake of her Italian bob. "And I
wouldn't have any girl who wishes to be a sculptor, or any other kind of artist, forget them. If
you wish to become an artist, you must take time
for training and that costs money." She studied
a year in Boston under Bela Pratt. She worked
two winters in New York under James Earl
Fraser of the New York Art Students' League.
One valuable summer she was a student of
Charles Grafly, pre-eminent in portrait
sculpture.

"Good sculpturing," said Brenda Putnam,

"depends on so much more than inspiration."
The brick-red of her velvet sport-dress was less
defiant than her voice. And the body from which
it issued was so small! Her eyes were black and
large and sparkling.

"There are many mechanical considerations.
First, there's the armiture—a delicate frame-
work, difficult to make, which goes into the too
malleable modelling clay. There is the plaster
case. Each material has very special limitations
which must be kept in mind. Marble, for instance,
is brittle. That is why Michael Angelo said that
a marble statue should be so solidly constructed
that no projection could break off if the thing
were rolled down hill! When I'm working for
marble, I think marble. When I'm working for
bronze, I think bronze."

Present-day sculptors have the good fortune
to work in plastiline or clay, their original figures
being converted into marble or bronze by a
modern machine which measures and cuts and
reconstructs. But Brenda Putnam is not always
sure that this is a case of good fortune. Her
instinct, she says, is to work first-hand in the
marble. No doubt she envies Praxiteles, one of
the great Greek sculptors of the Golden Age
who, like all his fellow-Greeks, cut and hammered
and chiselled the marble just as it came, naked,
from the quarries. The challenge of working in

stone! The thrill of conquering, beautifully, a resistant marble slab!

"Some things are made too easy for us these days," said Miss Putnam and I saw in her staunchness something of the ancient Spartan woman who had a dream to express—in rock.

And then she laughed, as she always laughs at the tail-end of her gravity.

"But what I said is true. A great deal of menial work goes with inspiration, if the inspiration is worth a scratch. Harold Bauer, the musician, says, 'Don't count on inspiration.' That's right—don't *count* on it. Why, sometimes I feel like shouting with Charles Grafly, 'I'm no sculptor, I'm a brick-layer.' "

Brenda Putnam, a brick-layer, Brenda Putnam, who plays her own grand piano with almost professional power, who draws delightful pictures in black and white for a child's version of *Pilgrim's Progress!* But I understood her point. She was thinking of the many, many hours of patient, persistent manual labor which must go into the making of a beautiful piece of sculpture. Without that labor, the sculpture is impossible. Manual labor follows inevitably upon inspiration if the sculptor is to realize his dreams in visible form.

"Come," said this paradoxical person, "and look at my babies."

We walked down three steps to the work-shop.

I went a little fearfully. Babies in plaster, I thought, would be wholly without appeal. But these were cuddlesome. The famous little *Sundial Figure,* riding a sea-horse, had wild hair and innocence and creases in his fat neck and a rambunctious big toe. The little *Peter* was all wonder and baby delight. A faun was just escaping from a garden with an armful of stolen flowers. Over here was a droll little fellow not yet a year old. Over there was a portrait of Master Desmond O'Hara, Miss Putnam's three-day-old nephew. He is, apparently, the youngest human being who ever went into marble. So wizened, so helpless—yet, in potentiality, a man.

"I never have enough of them," she exclaimed, including them all in a sudden gesture. "I like to create them. I enjoy arranging them in exhibitions, especially outdoor exhibitions where I may place my fountains in lovely open spaces or where my nymphs may peek out from the bushes. And I enjoy selling them, too—because aside from the fact that I earn my living in this way, I like to think that other people really are enjoying them.

"Sometimes I think that I should like to give all my time to my own work here in my studio. Yet I enjoy teaching my classes, too, especially when my students are truly appreciative of beauty."

"Most women sculptors are weak in technique,"

went on Miss Putnam when we were again
ensconced in our comfortable seats before the
fire. "But it is not entirely our fault. As yet, we
don't have the same opportunity as men. After
a man has learned to model the nude figure in a
school of sculpture, he can go into the studio
of some great sculptor. He serves, in other words,
his apprenticeship. He is like a medieval apprentice who hired out to a medieval master. He
learns, in this way, what no school teaches—
drapery, lettering, columning and what not. He
sweeps the floor; he arranges the folds of a gar-
ment; he makes the plaster casts. But women, you
see, are not accepted by men as apprentices.
Women get in the way! So to learn these techni-
calities, we must teach ourselves. But it takes
stamina."

Yes, and will-power. Brenda Putnam has both.
When she was asked to do the bas-relief of
Howells, for instance, she realized she knew
nothing about either bas-relief or lettering. They
just hadn't taught her those essentials in Boston
and New York. Was she daunted? No! She read
books on the subject, visited the museums, and
made a few experiments herself. In the end, she
knew the fundamentals of bas-relief, and put
them into brilliant practice. The result is this
sagacious-looking William Dean Howells.

The same courage caused Charlotte Brontë
to finish her novels, even though the odds were

all against her. If she couldn't write openly, she could write in secret and hide the manuscript in her sewing basket!

"Yes," went on Brenda Putnam, "determined women are making their way in all the arts—in writing, in music, in painting, in dancing. And I am proud of our women sculptors for I know against what difficulties they have won. Laura Gardine, Malvina Hoffman, Gertrude Vanderbilt Whitney, Evelyn Longman Batchelder—their work is distinguished."

I glanced about the room. On every side stood the work of a woman who sees beauty. In the up-curve of branches, in the majestic lift of skyscrapers, in the bend of a back or a knee. For her, beauty is everywhere.

"What a satisfaction," I cried, "to be able to put those lovelinesses into permanent form!"

"Yes," said Brenda Putnam, and for a moment I saw the artist in her flare up. Then she added with her characteristically dry humor: "But oh, the agony of seeing your mistakes in marble or bronze!"

"Still," I questioned, "you wouldn't be anything but a sculptor, would you?"

"No," she said earnestly, "I wouldn't."

ALICE FOOTE MacDOUGALL

*A girl who was a debutante
and who never expected
to enter business*

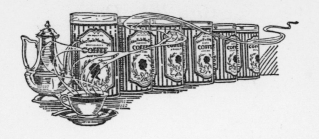

ALICE FOOTE MACDOUGALL

"I HAD three children," said Alice Foote MacDougall.

It was not the answer I had expected when I asked Mrs. MacDougall how it happened that she entered the coffee business. But she, herself, is unexpected. There where I had thought to find shrewdness only was something very human. One of the most successful business women in New York is essentially a mother: first and last and in between, Alice Foote MacDougall, dealer in wholesale roasted coffee and owner of restaurants, is a mother. Her ingenuity to her is mother-wit, her power of organization mother-tactics, her artistry mother love.

"Yes, my children are responsible for my business career. If it hadn't been for them, I should never have entered it," she said and tinkered with the orange beads against her blue serge dress. "This is my daughter," pointing to the photograph of a lovely young person. "And my

239

sons," pointing toward the photographs of two young men. All three were framed in silver. I looked at the door of the dingy office near the New York water front. "Alice Foote Mac-Dougall and Sons, Inc.," it read. "Dealers in Coffee."

The ramshackle office was in odd contrast to the delicate woman who dominated it. But the life of Alice Foote MacDougall has been one contrast after another. Her grandfather, Stephen Allen, was mayor of New York. Like most society girls, she never went to college. Yet today, trigonometry or no trigonometry, she makes her calculations as swiftly and as accurately as any coffee-man on the water-front. And they respect her. She never cheats them; she never asks for favors; she never says by her actions, "Handle me gently: I am a woman." Her philosophy is the philosophy of the woman who accomplishes. "In a world of men," she declares, "I must accept the hazards of a man's world. Else how can I hope for the same advantages?"

She says it gravely, and with conviction.

"Do you find it difficult," I asked her, "to compete with men?"

"Men are men and women are women," said Alice Foote MacDougall. "But in the business world they are neither. They are merchants or doctors—or jobbers in coffee. I buy. I sell. And I forget that I am a woman. Completely forget."

She spoke vigorously, and I became aware that a person can be both vigorous and gentle at the same time. Here was a woman capable of making clear-cut decisions. But a woman of charm. No wonder hundreds—no, thousands of people storm the upstairs and the downstairs of her one, two, three, four restaurants. No wonder.

How did those restaurants happen? She had mentioned roasted coffee, and a grandfather, and children. But none of these things explained the terra cotta walls of an Alice Foote MacDougall establishment, nor the Italian pottery, nor the delicious butterscotch pie up to its neck in whipped cream.

"Tell me," I begged.

And she told me.

"It is simple enough," she said. "You know how one thing leads to another. My business career really started for me long before I dreamed of entering it. My husband was a jobber in green coffee. From the time we were first married, I took great interest in his work. It was a fascinating world to me. Every night I plied him with questions about what he had been doing during the day. He used to discuss all his problems with me. I always knew his plans and how he proposed carrying them out. And the day came when I was more than grateful for this interest of mine.

"When I was forty, he died. I had three small

children who must be fed, housed and given education and much beauty. I was absolutely on my
own. And I resolved, from the first, to support
my family and ask no favors. It was a challenge.
Coffee was my salvation. For I decided to go on
with my husband's business.

"I soon found, however, that even though I
had talked with him in such detail about his work,
doing it myself was another matter. Much
remained to be learned. Every day seemed to
me so packed with details that I felt I couldn't
stop to think for one second or I would never
catch up with what had to be done. There was the
mail to be got through with, the orders to be
attended to, people to be seen. And very quickly
I saw there was much, much to be learned about
coffee. How could I stop to learn, to think? Yet
I knew I must or I could never develop the
business.

"In time, I did get the details organized. I
became acquainted with the people who were
working with me. I knew what each could be
counted on to accomplish. I knew what all of us
together must accomplish if the business were to
continue. It took months of hard work. But in
the end I was able to look about me—and think.

"We were dealing in green coffee in bulk. I
studied the situation and decided to try selling
roasted coffee by mail order. I spent many evenings reading everything I could find about

coffee, the various kinds, where each was grown, what the special distinction of each was. To learn each flavor, I drank coffee until I could recognize every kind. And I resolved to secure the most delicious coffee on the market for those who would come to me to buy.

"Business methods fascinated me. I talked with every successful business man whom I knew, whether he was in the paint business or the furniture business or the dress business. I wanted to see how each one went about his work, for I had grasped the fact that all business has certain factors in common. You must know your product— that is, what you have to sell, no matter what it is. You must make your product excellent. You must know why it is excellent, in order to tell others about it and sell it to them. And, in selling it and delivering it, you must render service. You must make them glad they bought of you not only because your product is good but because they receive it promptly and in good condition and because they can rely on your word. Whatever you promise, you must do. These are the fundamental principles of business, as I have learned them."

She paused.

"And the restaurants?" I reminded her.

"They followed just as naturally as my other ideas," she replied. "Green coffee in bulk had led me, you see, to roasted coffee by mail order.

Roasted coffee by mail order led to hot coffee over a counter. Coffee over a counter led to selling coffee accessories like coffee pots and percolators. Coffee do-dads led to the most beautiful pottery in the world which, to me, is Italian. And then, the Italian restaurants. Do you see?"

"But the troubles," I ventured. "Weren't troubles thick along the way?"

She narrowed her eyes upon her own past.

"Yes. But I didn't ask for a perfect day. I asked for success. They never go together. I remember so well the cubby-hole in Grand Central where I proposed trying my experiment of serving hot coffee. It was bare and dingy, apparently without the slightest possibility of attractiveness.

" 'Before we open those doors, we've got to make this a place where people will *want* to come,' I said to myself. And we started to work. We decorated the walls. We bought the most attractive china we could find. But we did not forget that delicious hot coffee was our reason for setting up shop. We saw to it that it was delicious— and hot. Soon we were serving waffles, too, because our customers had asked for them. And people enjoyed our little place. They crowded in. It was not long before I was being greeted on all sides with, 'Why don't you take over a larger place?'

" 'Why not?' I was soon asking myself. And started my first restaurant.

"Business means, inevitably, competition. When I started, only one other firm in New York was dealing in roasted coffee, and it was cheap and 'hard drinking.' Now there are many firms. Every time I turn around, up springs another. Each struggles to dominate the market. And as for the competition in restaurants, everyone knows how many restaurants there are in New York. How do I meet this competition? By turning my mind away from it to the business itself.

"If I give people what they want in coffee and in restaurants, they will come to me. Business is a game. It demands everything in you. Three courses are open. You have a product. You can sell it at a lower price than your competitors. You can give a better quality for the same price. Or you can add service and good will to your article. I aim at the last two. An attitude of courtesy and conciliation—it is so important. I learned its importance in that first little coffee booth I operated. The day I forget its importance, I hope I am forced out of business."

I looked into her face, and knew she would never forget these self-found principles. Her eyes were much too bright and much too determined.

Determination must have been born in Alice

Foote MacDougall, together with the ability to
execute a dream and the kind of originality which
twists a liability into an asset. That cubby-hole
in the Grand Central Terminal had three walls,
all ugly. She looked upon those walls and des-
paired, but not for long. She began to think. And
she made the Coffee Court into something more
than a bare coffee counter. Eventually, there were
four Italian restaurants.

The delicate-colored and crumbling walls of
the Old World—what is lovelier? Terra cotta
brick, cracked cobblestones, brilliant peppers
hanging, redly, on strings and eager flowers
everywhere. . . . Mrs. MacDougall reproduced
faithfully the Italian details and the mellow-yel-
low effect. And the public! The public has
decided that soup drunk in an Alice Foote Mac-
Dougall restaurant is more than soup, and cauli-
flower with Hollandaise sauce eaten under her
Italian sky, more than a well-cooked vegetable.

I said:

"Do you remember how you happened to get
the Italian idea?"

Surely it wasn't suggested by the water-front.
That office, occupied so many years by Alice
Foote MacDougall, was as unlovely, as un-
Italian as possible. The stairs were rickety, the
ceiling was low, and the rooms were given over
to a kind of well-ordered chaos.

"I don't know," said the Very Capable Lady.

"I really don't know. Perhaps it was the pretty Italian pottery which I sold with my coffee. Perhaps it was the memory of some sun-covered wall in Florence. I only know that, once the idea had formed, it was what I wanted to do.

"And that," she said, "is my story."

"I have a question," I replied. "What suggestions have you for girls who are entering business today?"

"That is a very large request when you consider the hundreds and thousands of businesses and the hundreds and thousands of girls in them," she smiled. "But it comes down to a few points, after all. Business is something which extends into every city and town of our country. The girl who is interested in it can enter a store or an office almost anywhere and set to work. If some special kind of enterprise or any certain kind of business surroundings attract her, she should do her best to secure an opening there. As regards her future, much depends on the nature of the opening itself, and much depends upon the girl's own ability and what she makes of her opportunity.

"A young woman of my acquaintance declared she wanted to go into insurance. Her family smiled at the idea. Where had she got that notion, they asked her. She didn't know where she had got it. She only knew she had it. Having, besides, a great deal of common sense and knowing that as yet she had little to offer any insurance company either in the way of training or business experience, she attended a commercial school long enough to learn filing. Then she secured a position as file clerk in an insurance company of recognized standing. From the first she kept her eyes and her ears open for everything about insurance that she could possibly learn. She took books from the public library. She talked with insurance salesmen. She examined the papers that passed through her hands. And in time announced to her surprised chief that she wished to try the selling of insurance. Which she did. In other circumstances, she might have attended one of the courses in selling insurance which some companies offer. Young women are doing this today. But this happens to be the way this particular young woman went at it."

Mrs. MacDougall paused reflectively, then continued, "But any young woman, starting out, finds herself confronted with much that confronted me in my coffee business, that day so long ago. She will have to learn what needs to be done and how to get it done in an orderly and systematic manner. And she must learn to adjust herself to all kinds of people. With this start, if she has business ability and circumstances are favorable, she can go on to acquiring a knowledge of the business which is going on around her, later, perhaps, branching out either there or elsewhere.

"I would not convey the idea, however, that every young woman is destined to become head of a business, or head of a department. There are, after all, but few heads compared to the great number at work. Nor would I even suggest the thought that every opening in business is splendid. It isn't. There are many blind alleys. And it sometimes requires a girl's utmost ingenuity and strength, not to mention money, to venture out, if she is to extricate herself and to find a real opportunity. Too many girls are permanently side-tracked in business blind alleys, and that is a very real tragedy in our business world. But I do say that more rests with a girl's own alertness than many realize. And with the variety of work which is carried on in the business world as a whole, it is often possible for the alert girl eventually to find that which approximates her capabilities, her interests and her strength.

"Why, think of the variety of work right here in my own business! I have young women stenographers, young women office managers, young women who sell the pottery and coffee at retail, young women who act as hostesses in the restaurants seeing that people are promptly and comfortably seated, young women who are waitresses, and I buy articles which have been made by young women. In one day's work I touch, I would say,

at least twenty-five kinds of work which girls
are doing and may do in business. But no matter
what a girl does——"

She paused. I waited.

"Let her never expect the perfect day nor the
perfect job," said Alice Foote MacDougall.
"There aren't any."

MARY KINGSBURY SIMKHOVITCH

A girl who liked folks
—and music
—and books

MARY KINGSBURY SIMKHO- VITCH

IF, when she was fifteen, you had asked Mary Kingsbury what she most enjoyed she could not have told you. She might have said, "My music." But then, remembering something else, she would have stopped, for there were her books. Yet mentioning books, she would have hesitated again, for there were people. How she did love folks!

Mary's father was on the staff of the Governor of Massachusetts and many fascinating guests came to enjoy the generous hospitality of the Kingsbury home. Cheeks rosy from a game of ball with the girls down the street, Mary was always glad if company was there when she came in. Best of all was the fact that most of their visitors treated her as somebody, including her in their conversation, often even asking her opinion on some matter under discussion. Being with people certainly was fun!

And yet—there was her music. The father who was her pal on larks at her grandfather's farm was her special comrade in music. When he sang in his lyrical voice, Mary played his accompaniments. And the evenings were not few when she and he sat up gorgeously late, to sing and to play. It is not recorded whether the rest of the family slept!

Yes, music was entrancing—and yet, there were books. Mary's mother loved books and to her young daughter she communicated a love of them no less deep than her own. Books from the library in the Boston suburb where they lived, the family's books, her own books in her own room, these, too, were a cherished part of Mary's life.

But which she most enjoyed, she couldn't have told.

One can think of many things which, as she grew older, a girl like Mary could find to do, to do well and to greatly enjoy in the doing. Perhaps that which most of those around her in her girlhood naturally thought would attract her was music. One music teacher, especially, had this in mind for her, a teacher so wise and entertaining that to this day Mary Kingsbury Simkhovitch cannot mention her without an affectionate light

in her eyes. For this teacher did far more than
show Mary the technique of finger exercises. She
brought her books about great musicians. She
played duets with her. She took her to concerts.
She taught her to read orchestral scores. And
with it all, she gave the young girl a glimpse
into the infinite beauty of music and the dreams
of our great composers who have brought us that
beauty for our own.

Yes, perhaps Mary would have chosen music,
after all, but for an overwhelming discouragement she soon met. In time, she had another
teacher, quite different. One week this teacher of
opera would tell her that her voice was one of
great promise, and the girl would go away filled
with happiness. The next week, this same teacher
would throw up her hands in despair, assuring her
pupil that her voice was quite hopeless. Bewil-
dered, Mary nevertheless persisted until at length
the discouragement became too great. And she
turned elsewhere, always, however, to cherish her
deep love and appreciation of music.

It was a clear, brisk autumn day when I
crossed the teeming street in front of Greenwich
House, on my way to talk with Mary Kingsbury
Simkhovitch. I knew that for twenty-five years
she has acted as director of this settlement house
—Neighborhood House, she prefers to call it
—with its clubs and its classes and its nursery

school and its music school and its many other activities. I myself had once come there to see exquisite Christmas pantomimes acted by the children of the neighborhood in the Greenwich House Children's Theater. Again I had come to see an exhibition of colorful pottery, made in the pottery room.

But I had never before come to ask Mrs. Simkhovitch how it was that she had found this work, so vital to others, so satisfying to herself.

Serenely the brick building that is Greenwich House rises above the honkings and the confusion that is Barrow Street, New York City. Widely its doors swing in welcome to the men and the women and the boys and the girls who crowd the sidewalks there. And friendliness greets you when you, yourself, step inside. No matter who you are, they are glad that you have come.

I enjoyed the few moments' wait while the woman at the desk in the hall announced me. Over in a corner, four little Italian boys were absorbed in a game. Their legs wound about the rungs of their chairs, their heads bumping over the table, they were oblivious to all passers-by, for it was *their* game, in *their* house, where they belonged.

An Italian woman with a very small black-eyed daughter, an Irish woman with a very small blue-eyed son hurried by me. The Italian woman opened a door and as the cavalcade passed through, I caught glimpses of a whole roomful of small boys and girls riotously engaged in something. Was it more pantomimes, I wondered. Another play for the Children's Theater? Whatever it was, it was fun and the mothers didn't want their children to miss it.

A house of friendliness, belonging to the neighbors.

"Come in," greeted Mrs. Simkhovitch, cordially welcoming me to her own apartment on the third floor.

I settled myself comfortably in a corner of a davenport, grateful after the noise of the city streets for this room of rest and peace, with its lovely old furniture, its fireplace, its pictures.

"Tell me about your plan," said she of whom I had come to ask questions.

And I knew at once that the friendliness of Greenwich House is none other than the friendliness of Mary Kingsbury Simkhovitch, that the feeling of belonging in the little Italian boys down by the door was real because she, herself, is real.

And I knew it must be characteristic of her that before I could ask her about herself, she would speak first of this book.

"It is for girls," I said. "There are many girls who are interested in your kind of work, or would be if they knew about it. It will help them if they can hear how you came to do this and have your suggestions for those who are starting out in it today."

"You are sure it will help?" she asked, simply, directly.

"Very sure," I replied.

How has it all happened? Mrs. Simkhovitch smiled. "Just as things do happen in this world," she said. "Not all at once, not without a great many mistakes on my part. Nor without days that were so hard it seemed as though I couldn't go on. Yet, after all, one thing led to another, almost casually."

And she told me of fifteen-year-old Mary Kingsbury, the girl who liked music and books and folks. "Looking back," she continued, "I can see the real significance of much that happened when I was a young girl. I clearly remember, for instance, the first time I ever saw how the very poor really live. A Sunday school teacher took several of us to the city, one Thanksgiving time, to present a turkey to a poor woman. We arrived at the ugly tenement, climbed the stairs through refuse and at last entered a stone-cold room. Very self-consciously, we placed the turkey upon the table and left."

Unexpected amusement twinkled in Mrs. Simkhovitch's eyes at the recollection. "Imagine that!" she exclaimed. "No fire. Apparently noth-

ing there to build a fire *with*. And we depositing
an uncooked turkey triumphantly! But even if
ill-advised, that visit left a deep impression upon
me. It seemed so unfair to me that some people
should be forced to live as that woman was doing,
while I and my friends were so comfortable.

"It was a picture which was later to return to
me forcibly. But meanwhile, I continued with
my schooling, eventually graduating from Boston
University and entering teaching. I taught in a
high school but soon decided that I did not care
for it. The work was so rigid. There were too
many papers that had to be corrected." Mischiev-
ously, she leaned toward me. "Sometimes I threw
them all in the waste basket without looking at
them," she whispered.

"So, because I did not like it, I left teaching.
And because I did like books and study, I entered
Radcliffe for graduate work. It was at this time
that I did some church visiting among the poor
of Boston and the picture of our Thanksgiving
visit so long before came back to me. It seemed
to me that conditions were no better than they
had been then. And the more I saw of poor people and their ugly and uncomfortable homes, the
more disturbed I became over it.

"Why did we have such a state of affairs?
What was the cause of it? Was it necessary? I
thought there must be some reason for it all
and I wanted to know that reason. As college

girls do, I turned to my studies and my professors for the answer, especially to my courses in economics. And I found that the question I was asking about injustice was an age-old problem, one that stretched around the world. My history told me that it was an injustice which had always existed.

"It was bewildering. Yet I never doubted that I and my friends could do something about it! By that time, I remember, I was acting as leader of a club of colored girls. The Primrose Club, we called it. When I knew the girls well, they invited me to their homes and I became familiar with the way in which colored people were forced to live. I next made a far more disturbing discovery—that the very tenements which were so deplorable were actually owned by several of my fellow church-members."

Mrs. Simkhovitch paused, lost in memory. Then, continuing——

"I decided upon still further study," she said. "I wanted to know more and more and more, you see, of how the world as it is came to be. Undoubtedly, this was my mother in me, whose respect was unbounded for what books can give. So, being awarded a fellowship for foreign study, I went to Berlin, taking courses there chiefly in economics, and meeting Mr. Simkhovitch, who was also engaged in graduate study.

"Oh, how I loved the music in Berlin! And

how I did enjoy my study there. But I returned at the end of a year, to continue at Columbia University. Again my old question would not let me alone. I wished to engage in some practical work. Yet the visiting of the poor which I had done while a student was now not enough. I became convinced that the conditions which so distressed me could not be remedied by intermittent visits, by this plan or that plan made for people without consulting them. I came to feel that I must live among those in whom I was so deeply interested, getting acquainted with them as my neighbors, studying their desires and the things they themselves could do and wished to do.

"So I entered the College Settlement House. I often think of the group of seventeen and eighteen-year-old boys who used to meet with me there on Sunday evenings. They called themselves the Economics Discussion Club and how they did enjoy grappling with tough questions! They were splendid boys, now grown men whom I meet here and there. Just the other evening, after I had been broadcasting, one of them came up to me. He holds a distinguished position in the government service. His brother is a physician. Another former member of this club whom I recently saw is successfully associated with a Spanish-American business firm. His was a good mind and real ability and he has made good use of both through the years. As I looked at them, I contrasted their

surroundings now with those of the tenements of
their boyhood days. And I was happy to have
them tell me that there in our Economics Club,
they found something of vital help to them,
which has proved a useful part of their own
education.

"But to continue. From the clubs and the
classes and the too-busy days and nights of the
College Settlement House, I became head worker
of the Warren Goddard House in New York.
While I was there, Mr. Simkhovitch and I were
married. And more evenings than not, we used to
sit up late together, discussing plans.

"In three years, we decided to try out those
plans. And we came to Jones Street and settled
down among the people who interested us so
deeply. It wasn't different, however, from settling
down anywhere in a new place. We ran out to the
corner store. We gradually got acquainted with
our neighbors. We were invited to their parties
and their weddings. And we started a kindergarten. A kindergarten, because we realized that
there are few people who do not wish to give
children the best possible of everything, and so
we felt it would be welcomed.

"Little Willie Zimmerman came as our first
client. I can see him yet, the son of a nearby deli-
catessen proprietor. Willie tried us out, liked us,
came again. And Willie and Willie's mother
spread word of the games and the songs and the

paper cut-outs that Willie so ardently enjoyed. So more mothers came with more children and our kindergarten was launched.

"From the first, everyone concerned with Greenwich House had a share in making our plans: those of us who lived here or who came in to do the work, those of our friends who helped us raise the necessary money, and the neighbors themselves. Our aim was high. We wished to make this part of the city the best place in which to live and work. But just what to do in order to reach our aim was to be a matter of all of us working and making plans together.

"And that is the way it has come about. As soon as the neighbors realized our genuine interest, they told us what they wished to have for their part of the city. We organized the Greenwich Village Improvement Association, with Italian members and Irish members learning to work harmoniously together. And little by little we worked for, and got, such things as a library and a public bath. Those about us came to feel that Greenwich House was indeed theirs, until now we have a nursery school for the children of mothers who must go out to work; visiting doctors and nurses to give health examinations and to suggest remedies. And clubs innumerable! Of course the boys and the girls wanted their own clubs with singing and dancing and entertainments and discussions and summer camp

trips. And the grown-ups were not far behind
in organizing clubs of the kind that especially
appealed to them.

"It was natural, too, that others should want
classes of various kinds. English for the foreign-
born, for instance. And the arts—it has never
seemed enough to me for us merely to be well
and strong and living in comfortable homes.
There must be meaning in our lives, a responding
to beautiful things. Our music school has been
one answer to this. And our wood carving. And
our pottery."

"May I see some of it all?" I asked.

She led me to the room in which boys, under
the supervision of an Italian expert, were drawing and modelling and carving, like medieval
apprentices, for pleasure and to order. On
another floor girls of all ages were modelling
clay into pottery shapes, glazing it with Persian
blues, and bitter-berry orange, and Chinese red,
and firing it in the kiln preparatory to the selling.

Forgetting me, forgetting everything but the
glowing blue bowl before her, Mrs. Simkhovitch
stopped still . . . then, remembering, she smiled.
"Isn't it beautiful!" she said—and opened the
door for me.

And downstairs, in the nursery school, was
Juleen, with hair like young grape tendrils and
eyes as dark and as big as black grapes. Juleen
herself was no bigger than a minute. If that. But

she was big enough to sit in a little red chair, at a little red table, and drink her little jug of orange juice. Over it all, she made a little chuckling sound and held out her jug with no uncertain meaning to the nurse in charge.

"More," said Juleen, juicily. "More."

Back again in the quiet of the apartment, Mrs. Simkhovitch spoke of their music school, where some of the finest musicians of New York City give lessons at moderate cost to boys and girls of talent.

"Our pupils pay all that they can afford," she explained. "Just as everyone does, in any of our clubs or classes. But we do not turn away those of talent because they have not the money for the lessons."

The work of twenty-five years—the busy building—her book, *The Settlement Primer,* published by the National Federation of Settlements in Boston and giving so much of all that she herself has learned through the years—there still remained much that I wished to ask her. Yet I wished to know, too, how she would start out in this field of work that is hers, were she young, here and now.

Into the story, I injected my question. "If you were a young girl today, Mrs. Simkhovitch," I said, "how would you start out in social work?"

"How would I start out today?" Mrs. Simkhovitch smiled. "Perhaps it would be better for me

to answer another question and that is—how
does any girl who is interested in this kind of work
start out? I would say that whether she wishes
to be a worker on a playground or a visiting
nurse or a club leader in a neighborhood house
such as this or a church visitor or a personnel
worker in some factory or store, she should ask
herself honestly, 'Do I enjoy being with people?
Am I really interested in them?' If what seems
romantic in the work attracts her, but if the
thought of being among people so constantly
annoys her, I would say that social work is not a
wise choice for her.

"But if she does enjoy folks, what then? Any
one of a number of plans! In general, I think she
should get the best and most thorough education
which she can afford. The more she has within
her, the more wisely she will be able to go among
people, working out with them plans which will
make their living broader, more healthful and
more enjoyable.

"If she can go to college, so much the better.
But whether she goes to college or whether she
does not—and a college degree is not necessary
for entering the field of social work—she should
learn before she starts how to do some one thing
well. Just as the young woman who wishes to
enter the world of business has a definite opening
wedge if she is proficient in stenography and
typing, so the girl who is interested in social work

can create an opportunity for herself if she knows folk dances and games and can direct a group in them; if she can lead clubs of girls and boys; if she can assume charge of the production of plays; if she is trained in public health work; if she has learned how to conduct special investigations—if she can do well any one of a wide variety of activities.

"If she wishes to develop a specialty, she can do so in the many schools which give special courses of training. Dancing and the directing of games and sports are offered in schools of recreation and physical education. Courses in public health work are offered in an increasing number of educational institutions in this country. And so on.

"If a girl thinks she will be interested in carrying on special investigations for a charity organization society or a church, if work such as that of a probation officer in a court appeals to her, there are schools which offer training in it. Such work is commonly called 'case work' and practise in it, as well as instruction in its deeper significance, is to be had in the schools of social work in Philadelphia, New York City, Chicago, Atlanta and elsewhere. There are certain requirements for entering these schools which may be easily ascertained.

"There are openings, too, for the young woman who can direct the work of others, the good administrator. This week, we are adding to our staff a new head of our art work. She herself is a writer and an artist, so that she understands what those under her will be doing. She has had excellent experience as an executive secretary so that she knows how to be in charge of others.

"Since social work includes so many kinds of activity, it is difficult to mention them all. But further possibilities occur to me. Suppose a girl is especially interested in Y. W. C. A. work, in church work, in the work of the Camp Fire Girls or the Girl Scouts, in the club work which is carried on by the Department of Agriculture in Washington, in playgrounds—the national organizations sponsoring these fields have national headquarters and special training courses for their workers. All that a girl need do who is interested in any one of them is to write to those national headquarters, inquiring about the qualifications necessary for a young woman who wishes to enter their work as a profession.

"So I cannot say to girls that social work requires a college degree or training in a school for social work. The question resolves itself into the girl herself and what she can do and wishes to do. If she is still in high school or college and is thinking about this field but wondering whether, after all, she really wishes to enter it, she may try herself out. As a member of a Camp

Fire Girl, Girl Scout, Girl Reserve or club group, a girl learns how to work and play with others. She learns to develop herself as a leader. Later, she may go to a settlement house or to her church or other organization and serve as a volunteer leader of a group. Here at Greenwich House, we have many such volunteer leaders who have not yet completed their college studies but who think they may wish to enter work of this kind when they do graduate. The hours they spend here each week with their boys and girls are not only helping us but are showing them something about themselves and what they can do. If, later, they decide to enter this work as a profession, they will be making that decision on a foundation of actual experience.

"More and more, I am hearing that girls still in school are spending their summer vacations in various kinds of work, experimenting with this and that, trying to discover what they best like to do and for what they are best fitted. It is a splendid plan! And one that is readily put into practice in social work what with summer camps conducted everywhere by settlements and other organizations, in which a girl may act as counselor; what with playgrounds always eager for assistants; what with the summer play schools in our large cities. There are many opportunties to be found by the girl who is alert.

"Yet, after all, to do any one kind of work well is *not* enough in this field. In social education, as I prefer calling it, there must be human understanding. Without this understanding, it is arid. But with it—" she paused, her eyes alight.

"With it," she concluded, "there is neighborliness."

MARIA JERITZA

A girl who could
sing but who
was very shy

MARIA JERITZA

THE gods were lavish when they made Maria Jeritza. A great beauty, a consummate actress, a voice out of heaven—all meet in one international opera singer. It is too much. She is Brunhilde, turned gentle. She is Juno, made mortal.

Am I extravagant in my praises? No doubt. But I have heard Jeritza sing *Thais* in the Metropolitan Opera House and I have talked to her in her suite at the St. Regis. Both times she was queenly—on the stage, in a flowing costume and a crown; in her apartments, in a simple dress and no make-up. Perhaps I liked her a little better in private. The dramatic soprano voice which stirred, first Europe, then America, was locked away in her throat. But to compensate, there was informality coupled with a very blond gaiety. I remember wondering, on that afternoon, whether the prima donna had knowingly chosen the sherry-red of the curtains, rug, and upholstered chairs as a background for her gold-and-white self. No, I decided—Maria Jeritza is too natural to calculate her background. Nevertheless, the sherry-red, the tall Viennese vases, the long mirror, and the red china berries on little china bushes were a delightful setting for her loveliness.

I asked her the old, old question, "Did you dream, as a child, of grand opera?"

Her blue eyes looked between the fringe of her dark lashes. Her hands moved expressively.

"I dreamed much," she said with a slight Austrian accent. "In Moravia, where I was born, everybody sings in the schools and in the church. But I took my singing very see-riously."

"Yes?" said I. "And that was——?"

"When I was twelve," said Madame Jeritza. "I took private lessons from a Professor Krejci at that time, and he taught me the very first principle of singing—never to scream and never to force a tone. When I was fourteen, I began lessons with Professor Auspitzer of Brunn, my home town. In between my singing, I pretended that I was a great actress performing in the fairy tales which I and my old calico doll enacted together. I was the heroine. My cat was the wicked ogre. Yes, yes, I dreamed much. And at fifteen, I had a very great ambition to go on the stage."

She told me, then, of her shyness. If any stranger listened to her singing, a nervous fear contracted the muscles of her throat and shut out the sound. How could she ever give an audience to a manager? Professor Auspitzer solved the problem by concealing, behind something or other, the director of the Olmutz Theatre, while the eighteen-year-old Maria ran through her repertoire of opera selections. At the end of this inadvertent exhibition, the director emerged and engaged the girl for his opera!

At dress rehearsal she had stage-fright. But the stage-fright somehow fell from her when she stepped forward in her first public appearance. She was a success. She was an instant success.

After five months in Olmutz, she went to Vienna. When the director of the Volksoper heard her sing Micaela's aria from *Carmen*, he was even more hasty with his contract than the Olmutz director. There was no mistaking the extraordinary quality of this voice.

The career of Maria Jeritza from then on was a fairy tale more astonishing and more real than the fairy tales which she dramatized as a child. Because a broad education is necessary for the highest attainments in grand opera, she persevered in her studies. History—an opera star must know the historic setting of each opera, if her characterizations and her costumes are to be accurate. Languages—an opera star must sing in all the major languages, German, French, Italian and English and, if her singing is to escape being a blur of syllables, enunciate perfectly. The art of acting and the art of dancing are often as important in opera as singing. It was Max Reinhardt who taught Maria Jeritza how to handle her body on the stage.

"We are required to do more and more acting," she said. "A prima donna used to sing an aria, and let it go at that. . . . To-day she is called upon to act highly emotional roles."

I remembered Fedora and Marguerite and Tosca—memorable for that golden voice, filling, for the first time, the Metropolitan Opera House, and the avalanche of roses which fell at her feet. No European capital had given her a more cordial welcome. And that welcome has never worn thin. Since the historic year of her first American appearance, Jeritza spends every winter, from November to February in New York. America, which is not preëminently a music-loving nation, senses the deep sincerity of the woman and loves her.

But sunlight casts, somewhere, a shadow. Jeritza, too, has known her shadows. In the beginning, her mother opposed her going on the stage; her brothers and her sisters laughed at her dream-

ing. Once, in Hamburg, the critics were scathing
in their denunciation of her voice. In Vienna she
was tempted by an offer of a career on the legitimate stage. Joan of Arc was the role which a
manager flourished before her—and which she
rejected.

Even her world-wide triumphs did not end her
troubles. The life of an opera star has its distinct
disadvantages. Self-denial is all along the way.

"I am never master of my time," said Jeritza.
There was no petulance in her voice, only an
infinitesimal regret. "My manager maps out my
dates one year, two years, three years ahead. I
go about my business like a soldier or an official
fulfilling his duties. If I don't eat well, sleep
well, and exercise sufficiently, my voice suffers.
But the worst part of being an opera singer is
being continually an object of public curiosity.
I cannot go shopping, or attend the theater, or
walk on the streets, but I am stared at."

Poor woman—for she is, after all, just a
woman. How painful to have people forever
pointing, and whispering, "Look! There's
Jeritza!" and asking, "Do you think the hair on
her head is false?"

"I can never stop work on my voice nor my
studies," she went on. "Since I began my stage
appearances, I have studied harmony, counter-
point, canon and fugue, composition and orches-
tration. In each opera, I must be familiar with

every note my partner sings as well as with my own role. I must know what the orchestra is to do, for how could I tell them to tune up or down if I didn't know all the opera, as well as the difficulties and the possibilities and the technical capacities of each instrument?"

Jeritza in the flowing robes, Jeritza in the queenly crown and the lavish setting of the Metropolitan—and Jeritza studying diligently. Days of hard work. Years of constant striving. Since she was twelve, she has persisted in this one art. Until she gives her last public performance, she must think chiefly of it, if she is to maintain the high quality of her singing.

"What of the girls who wish to enter music?" I asked her.

She spoke at once of teachers. "Teachers have so much power to hurt or to help," she said. "In vocal work, wrong exercises can ruin a voice. Correct exercises strengthen it. So with the piano, so with the violin. Pity the young musician who learns incorrectly. Good teaching—every girl who studies music should have it."

"And what then?" I asked.

Again her hands stirred gently in her lap. "More study. And more work. It is for the girl herself to discover what next. If she is a singer, she will learn the quality of her voice through her studies. In time she will know whether it is for singing in a choir or on the concert stage or in the theater or the opera. It is so with the piano or the violin or other instrument. Everything depends on her talent and how she develops it."

"But there are so few who can do what you have done, Madame Jeritza," I said.

She considered it frankly. "Yes," she replied. "The opera is for the so very few. Ah, the disappointments I have seen. So many work. So many dream. And so few succeed as they have dreamed. But what if a girl is not what you call a star? Perhaps she will become a most excellent teacher."

We talked of music in Europe and in America. Madame lamented the fact that America, unlike Europe, has no opera houses in her small-sized towns.

"There should be more music, lovely music everywhere if America is to have many beautiful musicians and composers. To listen when you are a child does so much for you. Music becomes what shall I say—part of your very life. Much music enters into the very soul. And when it is in the soul—ah!"

"What role do you like best?" I asked tritely.

She smiled. But she did not answer my question. Instead she said:

"If I don't like a part I don't sing it. How can I render a role beautifully if I hate that role? An audience is quick to sense lack of sympathy in a singer and quick to resent it." Thus did she refuse to name specially a single-beloved aria. They are all beloved!

She was moving toward the door now, tall and self-possessed. A great success bestows upon a woman—if she is made of enduring stuff—not only a sense of fulfillment but an invulnerable poise. For a moment she stood motionless against the sherry-red of the full-length curtain.

Then, "Goodbye," she said graciously, and was gone.

I pushed my way through the crowd on the sidewalk below and thought of Jeritza's days. Days of rigid requirements, of never ceasing to pay the price for excellence in her art. Moments of supreme satisfaction because of what those days enable her to do.

Jeritza—the genius. But what of those who are not?

Impulsively I turned down a side street. As I approached a certain door, a small boy bounded out and down the steps.

"Goodbye, Teddie," said a warm friendly voice.

"Goodbye," returned Teddie with a grin.

I went in. "How was Teddie's music lesson this time?" I inquired of my friend.

She shook her head. "Pretty poor. Teddie is not a musician, you know."

"Don't you get frightfully bored?" I asked, although I knew better.

She reproved me with a look. "Why, no. My pupils interest me, even the Teddies. I know it looks boring to you, my sitting beside that piano day after day, listening to the struggles of beginners. To you, not to me. That is the difference. And here is another difference—I must admit that your enthusiasm for writing, your working hours to find just the right word, looks like nothing but hard labor to me!"

"Oh, no!" I protested.

"Exactly," said my friend. And we laughed together.

"I have been to see Jeritza," I told her.

"A sincere artist. And now I suppose you are thinking of the price of achievement and how hard she must work to hold what she has won and to go on?"

I started. "Yes, I am," I admitted.

My friend leaned forward. "Of course she works hard! Of course we all work hard. I do. You do. The only thing that is different is the degree of our talent. Jeritza is simply paying the price everyone must pay for doing something well. She is outstanding because she has outstanding talent. But there are many girls——"

I interrupted. "That is what I wish to ask you," I said. "What about the many girls who are talented musically? You were born in the

United States. You know what such a girl must do to develop her talent. Or *shall* she develop it?"

"Develop it? Yes, if she wishes to and can afford to. If a girl is naturally attracted to music, she will enjoy developing the ability that she has. And it may be she will find in it her permanent work. That was my experience. As you know, I found my piano teaching.

"From the start, a girl must face the necessity for musical training. A good teacher is essential. Girls are too often handicapped by poor teachers. Yet it is sometimes very difficult to learn just who is a good teacher. In a small town, the choice is limited. In a city, the number of teachers is bewildering. If only there were some sure method of finding your way to a good one! I can only suggest that a girl proceed carefully, perhaps consulting someone in whom she has confidence, such as a musician who is already doing excellent work—a pianist or an organist or a choir director.

"When she has exhausted the possibilities of musical training where she lives, there comes the question of going away for further study—and where. The department of music in her state university is an excellent source of reliable information for a girl, whether or not she plans to attend the university itself.

"How I wish I might warn every girl, who has saved her money and who plans to go to a city for her musical education, of the necessity for investigating the teacher or the school where she plans to study! Many unscrupulous teachers encourage a girl until her money is gone, then tell her that her voice or her playing talent has not come up to expectations. A good teacher does more than teach well. He evaluates the ability of his pupils. He tells a girl frankly when he believes her talent does not justify the investment of further time and money. Being interested in a certain kind of work never necessarily means that you can do it well. A girl must be ready to face facts.

"A musical education costs money. A girl needs it for her lessons from the outset. She needs it if she decides to study in Europe as I did. There are, to be sure, some musical scholarships which help with these expenses, when a girl can secure one. And it is possible to continue with her training in relays, studying for a certain length of time, then teaching for awhile in order to earn more money for more study. That has been my plan, Teaching—studying—teaching —studying. Even now I use part of my income for further study."

"And you chose teaching music because it appeals to you more than anything else?" I asked.

"Yes," she replied. "I never regret my teaching. I enjoy it. A teacher has such an opportunity to develop not only musical ability but musical appreciation. I shall never be able to make a musician of Teddie, I know. But he will come to enjoy music and to discriminate in it, I feel sure. And the more people we have in this country who enjoy and discriminate, the greater will be the demand for lovely music in America and the greater will be the opportunity for splendid musicians and the better music we shall have. It is a cycle—and the Teddies are needed.

"But to return to my own choice. Concert work interests me, too, although I myself should never care to give my entire time to it. For that matter, most of the musicians of my acquaintance who play in concerts or who compose, also teach. Others give their entire time to teaching, either privately as I do, or on the staff of a public school, a private school, a normal school, or in the school of music of a college or a university.

"There are some doors that are still closed to women in the musical world. Women rarely play in our large orchestras, almost never direct one. Yet they may direct a chorus or a choir or an orchestra in a school, a church, a club or similar organization.

"Yes, there are opportunities for young women who are musically talented and trained. There are opportunities in public performance and composing as well as in teaching. And there will be still wider opportunities."

She spoke with conviction. She had, I knew,

met the hardships with which a girl who has but a limited amount of money is confronted in securing her musical education. But she does not regret her effort. She has her piano. She has her pupils. She has her occasional public performance. And there in her book-lined studio, with its welcoming fireside, she finds satisfaction in what she is doing.

The same satisfaction which I felt in Jeritza.

You

A Girl
who is wondering
about herself

YOU

What about you?

It is interesting to read about women who are doing all kinds of things and to know what they were like when they were girls, yet after all—"What about me?" you ask.

"I am different from every one of them," you think. "It was easy for them. They had talent. I haven't a sign of it. And as for being a genius——!"

Isn't it just possible that your idea of talent is too limited? For talent means more than ability to write or sing or draw well. There is a talent for system, for keeping things in order. The girl whose bureau drawers are always neat, who never forgets an appointment has this talent and may make an excellent office manager or secretary. There is a talent for people, for getting along with them, for inspiring them, for making them believe in themselves and for teaching them. This talent is of greatest use in social work and in teaching. There is a talent for growing things which can lead girls to successful work in some kind of agriculture.

Often a girl is unconscious of the very thing in herself which should point the way for her to her logical profession. One girl was exceedingly popular with her small nieces for her story-telling and the delightful little games which she originated. But the idea of becoming a kindergarten teacher never occurred to her until someone else suggested it. And she often wonders, now, how she could have been so blind, for today her small pupils, as well as she, herself, greatly enjoy her kindergartening.

It is for you to discover yourself, to try yourself out in as many ways as you can. Your experience as a high school girl is just as important and just as significant as any you will ever have. If you are a member of a Camp Fire Girl, Girl Scout, Girl Reserve or club group, take part in their various activities. Do not limit yourself to one or two. And as you work upon the badges or the honors, who knows but that you will discover an unsuspected ability in yourself? Almost without exception, each woman in this book has spoken of things which you, as a girl, may do in order to try yourself out in her particular field.

But this, of course, is only the start. What of

the training you must have? And how much will it cost? How can you find out just where and how you may enter the kind of work in which you are interested?

You realize that these questions must be answered and you feel truly discouraged because your problems seem so much more real and so much greater than those which these women faced when they were young.

If the achievement of these women seems easy to you, it is because in one book it has not been possible to tell the entire story of each. But if you will look back at what they have said of the way in which they got their start, you will find mention of, "It was necessary for me to earn money at once, so I———", "Three years later, I———", "Then in five years, I———"

Can't you imagine what happened during those years? There were mistakes and hard work and discouragements, as well as days of accomplishment. Indeed, accomplishment itself is made up of failures and discouragements, as well as successes. If you could talk with each of these women yourself, you could know intimately of all that those days and years held for them and you would realize that while you are different from every one of them and that while your problems are your own and nobody else's, nevertheless what you must do and what they did are not so different, after all.

By no means all of them knew from the first what they wished to do. Some had special talent, to be sure. A few had genius. But others groped their way along, trying first this, then that. And here again you will find them mentioning years in their discovering. Eventually, some who had not realized that they had any special talent found that they did. Others have never discovered any. But they have found a kind of work and surroundings which appeal to them and where their interest in what they are doing and their persistence have brought them to their present position.

And just as you have your personal problems to face, so did each of them when they were girls, so have they today now that they are women. Some, as girls, were shy and hesitant and self-conscious. Some were impatient. Some had heavy responsibilities and could not use the money they earned for their own further training, but must give it to their families for rent and food and clothes.

In high school you are associated with all kinds of girls and boys. Some you like and some you do not, but you must continue to go to school with those who are there. You will find the same situation when you enter your work. And the girl who learns to get along with all kinds of people has a valuable asset in whatever she may decide to do.

The real responsibility for discovering yourself and for finding an opportunity rests with you, yourself. If there is something which you can do well, something which you enjoy doing, look around and see whether there is not a kind of work in which your special tastes and abilities are needed. The fields described in this book are but few of those which are open to women today. Every public library has books and magazines which will give you many more. Ask your librarian for them.

Talk with the vocational adviser in your school, if you have one; with your teachers; with women you know who are engaged in various kinds of work. Ask them the questions which were asked the women in this book: "How did you start? What are the qualifications necessary in a girl who wishes to do this work? What training should I have? Where can I get it? How much will it cost? What opportunities are apt to be open, once I am ready to start out?" Be your own interviewer!

As you talk with them, you may find that their advice and suggestions are different from those given here—concerning the same fields! This will give you a basis for comparison. What is suggested here may not be best for *you* in *your* circumstances. Each story is, after all, but that of one woman and so gives you only one way of entering and progressing in any particular field.

It is, however, the story of a woman who has achieved and so is significant to you.

It is never too soon for you to inform yourself about any field, especially since certain training may be required for entering it and you will then wish to be planning for that training. It is always important for a girl to secure her training in the best available school. Where shall you go? Where *can* you go? It may be necessary for you to take your training in the town where you live, because you cannot afford to go elsewhere. Make the most of what you have, remembering that there is always the possibility of later saving your money and continuing somewhere else. On the other hand, it may be possible for you to go to any school or college which will offer you the best training available. But what is the best school?

The girl who wishes to secure information of this kind may go to her teachers or the librarian in the public library. One list of such schools and colleges is published by the United States Bureau of Education. And other lists are available in books. A librarian will look up for you the names and addresses of the places which offer the training you desire, or she will tell you where you may go for further help. The registrar in your state university or in the normal school which is nearest you is ready to give you suggestions if you will tell what it is you wish to know. The graduates of schools are always willing to tell you about what they did there. Don't hesitate to ask for information!

But with the question of what training is necessary comes the inevitable, "How much will it cost?" Don't forget that many scholarships are available, which help in no small way with expenses. Ask about these scholarships and how you may apply for one of them. Remember, too, that new ways of earning money are constantly opening up for the student who wishes to go on with her education. Most colleges and many normal schools have "Self Help Bureaus" and the dean of any college or university will be pleased to tell you of the ways in which the students are helping to pay their own way. Positions are also open to students during their summer vacations. These are possibilities which should be considered by the girl who must face financial ways and means, with the encouraging thought that since other girls have done it and are doing it, why not you?

Don't overlook the fact, however, that the girl who earns her own way through college or special school must be a girl with excellent health. For it is not easy to pay your own way, at the same time keeping up with the class work of your courses. For this reason, some girls work for a year or two between high school and college, saving money and at the same time gaining experience in holding a position which serves them in good stead in earning money at college. One girl who was graduated from high school not long ago and who is now earning her way through college, attended a business college immediately upon completing high school. She then entered upon work as a stenographer, saving her money and gaining experience in stenography and typing. The money that she thus saved helped to make her freshman year somewhat easier and her experience gained for her a part-time position which she has now held for two years and which fits in with her college schedule.

Another plan which many college presidents consider wiser than for a girl to attempt to earn her entire way through a special school or college is that of borrowing money for the course. This is more widely customary in Europe than in this country, but already girls here are finding the plan feasible, repaying the debt when they have been graduated and have a salaried position. By this plan, their health is not so severely taxed. And if the amount borrowed is not too great, the time needed for its repayment is not discouragingly long.

"This is the kind of investment which business men make every day," said Dr. Henry Noble MacCracken, president of Vassar, recently. "Why shouldn't young women invest in their futures?"

For the girl who cannot, for the life of her,

discover any one thing which she can do especially well or any one thing which appeals to her more than anything else, there is the thought of the many other girls who have been in just that situation. Some have found it necessary to go to work. Others have tried staying at home, have decided that work would be more interesting and useful—and have started out.

To learn to do one thing well is an opening wedge. This opening wedge may be obtained in a trade school or in a business course. If a girl can type well, do filing or operate a machine, she has something to offer. A position awaits her. From this start, she can look about, possibly studying in an evening school to prepare for a better position, at the same time acquiring experience right where she is. And, like Mabel Stewart, she is quite likely eventually to find the atmosphere and the work which appeal to her.

After you have completed your training and entered upon your work, what then? You may like it—and you may not! If you are unhappy, study carefully to discover the reason and then decide what to do about it. You may have chosen the wrong thing for you. Marion Durell did, at first. Or you may merely be working in an uncongenial situation, with the work itself that which you wish to do. Before you make a change, decide which it is.

Or it may be yourself. Some girls expect to

find impossibly congenial surroundings. And they never will. Others are discontented when any part of what they do is distasteful. Every kind of work that exists has its "ornery" parts. As Alice Foote MacDougall says, "Don't look for the perfect job. There isn't any."

Ability to get along with all kinds of people is an asset. But there is such a thing as jealousy and you may meet it. Some jealous person may block your advancement. There is much beside the actual work itself which can make a girl unhappy.

No girl should forget that a change is possible. Neysa McMein changed her work. Gertrude Hawley did. Minna Hall Carothers did. But before you actually make a change, ask yourself —just why am I discontented? Is it my work? My surroundings? Or myself? Sometimes a girl can transform an unfavorable situation into a favorable one by being a more generous, a more understanding or a more efficient person.

Don't change hastily. And don't forget that a change is possible. Some girls are like grasshoppers, jumping from one position to another whenever they find something wrong with the position in which they happen to be at the time. Other girls plod on and on in uncongenial work, not taking time to apply their intelligence in analyzing what is wrong and what the best way to remedy it.

All along the way are new adventures and new problems to be solved and new difficulties and new successes—for that is the way of life.

Yes, you are a girl who is wondering about herself. But you are not alone. Girls in the Near East are wondering. Girls in Europe are wondering. Girls in South America. Girls in the Orient. And girls in all parts of the United States.

Everywhere, girls are confronted with a world vastly different from that which their grandmothers knew, vastly different from that which their mothers knew, as girls. You are the discoverer of yourself. And you are a discoverer of a new world. There has never been a time when it was more interesting and worthwhile to be alive.

But there is more before you than the discovering. There is the making. Whatever you decide to do, you will not be alone. Other girls will be with you, and men and women and boys. You will have your family, those whom you love and care for. And what you do—what other girls do—will be an important part in the making of a new world.

Because she knows a great deal about what girls everywhere are doing and what they are facing, we asked Miss Mary Van Kleeck to tell you about some of those things of which she thinks, as she looks out from the high windows of her office.

When Mary Van Kleeck was a senior in Smith College, she was awarded a fellowship from the College Settlements Association to investigate the number of hours which factory girls in New York were then working. She was attracted to the plan. She liked the idea of making investigations which would help girls to better the conditions under which they were employed. So she accepted the fellowship and became acquainted with girls in many different trades. She met them at their work. She talked with them in their clubs. She visited them in their homes. They liked her because of her friendliness and because they saw that she was interested in what they were doing.

Mary quickly realized that these girls were working too hard—sometimes thirteen hours in one day. She watched them lift heavy rolls of paper and realized that they couldn't possibly do it without harm to themselves. She learned of their poor pay and knew that they used that pay not only to buy food and clothes for themselves but for other members of their families.

And she wrote of what she found in order that others might help these girls to better the conditions of their work. Today, Miss Van Kleeck and others like her still work to extend yet more widely these better conditions which have gradually come for girls and women and men who are employed. But that has taken time.

Meanwhile, Mary Van Kleeck turned to the study of other kinds of work that girls and women were doing. When the Russell Sage Foundation took over the investigations, she became associated with the Foundation, enlarging her research to include the work of men as well as of women. During the war, it was Mary Van Kleeck who was summoned by the United States Department of Labor to act as director of the Women's Bureau.

And from this Women's Bureau to every plant engaged in war work in this country, where women and girls were employed, went her plans for the hours they could best work and the kinds of work which they could undertake without harm to themselves. For she knew that if the girls and women were harmed not only would the work itself suffer, but the children of whom these girls and women were to be the mothers would suffer. It was a responsibility for the present and for the future. And thousands of girls who never saw Mary Van Kleeck during those war days, who perhaps never even heard her name, owe much to her careful planning in Washington.

Today, back at the Russell Sage Foundation as head of the department of industrial studies, she finds time to act as trustee of Smith College and to go out to meetings of girls in many parts of the country. Because she is so deeply interested in girls everywhere, she has written to you.

To You, From Mary Van Kleeck

Do you want a career? What kind of work interests you? Must you work for a living? Is your first duty to your parents, or will you plan your vocation and, if necessary, leave home as freely as your brother?

You have read these stories of women who have been successful in many fields of work. Not all are famous, but all have been useful, all are today enjoying what they are doing, and several have achieved something quite original. Perhaps you have imagined yourself in the place of one of them, or all of them, one by one. You may have sung on the stage of the Metropolitan Opera House with Jeritza. You may have devoted yourself to the cause of social justice with Mary Simkhovitch. You may have coached a hockey team with Gertrude Hawley; nursed a sick patient with Marion Durell; written a story with Inez Haynes Irwin; or run a restaurant with Alice Foote MacDougall.

But you will soon close this book and, as you awake from your day dreams, you will ask, "What have these to do with me? How do their experiences help me? I am not like any one of these interesting women. I must be myself. But what is 'myself' and what work is *mine*?"

You are right. You must choose for yourself. But you are not the only girl in the world who must face the problem of choosing an occupation and of carrying it on after it is chosen. So I am writing to you today to suggest some things that are common to all girls, to tell you what others are thinking about the very questions which are puzzling to you.

I think one of the first things which you should realize is that there is no neat, simple rule by which you can decide on the work which you will most enjoy and which is best suited to the kind of girl that you are. You are living in a world in which the whole economic organization is changing. The very forms of work are changing, constantly. No field of work, no vocation remains exactly the same from one year to the next.

If I were to attempt to make a list of all possible kinds of work that you may enter, and to tell you what would be required of you if you were to enter each of them, it would take hundreds more pages than can be put into one book. And in the end, all that I could say would be that what I had told you was *approximately* true for the present moment. The important thing for you, the girl of today, to know is that vocations and all the conditions in which we live are changing. How to plan your life in a changing world, not how to fit your life into a fixed order of things, is your problem and mine.

Girls all over the world are meeting this same situation, not only on this continent but in all the countries of Europe and indeed in the Near East and the far Orient, just as their mothers are meeting it. The homes in which our great-grandmothers lived were far different from our homes today. Our great-grandmothers, helped by everyone in the household, spun the wool, made the clothes, made the soap, made the candles, cured the meat—in short, did many things which are today done for us in factories.

And when the work which was formerly done in the homes began to be done outside, at that moment the position of girls and women began radically to change. The home was no longer to be a place where food and clothing could be provided by the family for its own needs. And today no family lives to itself. Goods are produced on a large scale, outside the home.

You can readily see what this change means for us. Yesterday, the girl at home found her time entirely filled with the many activities there. Today, some girls, released from their great-grandmother's tasks, have too much leisure. Others go out from their homes to work for wages, making in factories the very articles which were formerly made at home. And in between these two groups of girls are those who are planning to enter the movement of women into the many tasks which society also needs— teaching, art, social service, civic work, medicine, law and other occupations outside the economic organization for the production and distribution of goods.

So it is that whatever the field of work in which you are interested, it is a changing field today as trains and boats and automobiles and airplanes and the radio bring different parts of the world closely together and your clothes and your food are supplied for you without the effort of making them on your part. You pay for them with the salary which you earn.

It is important for you to remember that all these changing economic conditions are drawing girls and women out from their homes and into the great field of work outside the home. Work for wages or salary is becoming less and less a matter of choice and more and more an inevitable part of the ways of life in the world about us.

In a sense, it is desirable that it should be so. Work is and always has been important to the happiness of everyone. Without useful work, a girl is incomplete, undeveloped—not the girl she can be and should be.

Although the many changes which I have mentioned are also influencing the world of work for men and boys, and although your brother is faced with your same problem of choosing what he is to do, of securing training for it and of deciding just where he shall enter it, you have another problem to face. You have the problem of what you, as a daughter, shall do about your vocation. Most often I call it "the problem of coördination," a large phrase but I think you will understand what I mean.

If you are still living in your parents' home, you are quite likely to be confronted with the question: "Shall I go to work *or* stay at home?" This confuses you. You are pulled here and there by circumstances. Some girls do not face the question, but go to work without any planning, in order that they may earn money to help out on the family's expenses. They take whatever position is at hand, with the result that their work is never the interesting or developing thing which it might be for them.

Or, if there is no real need for a girl to earn money, she may be led into believing that her parents need her at home, and she lets precious years slip by without developing her own talents and without preparing herself for useful work.

Every girl must face her own personal situation. Every girl must work out her own problem. Yet I suggest that you try to eliminate the *either or* from your own thinking. I suggest that you, as a girl, accept the idea that it is desirable for every woman, including yourself, to have a vocation. Let the question which you are trying to answer be no longer the "Either-or," but "How?"

Your parents have claims upon you but—*how* shall you fulfill your obligations as a daughter and at the same time enter the work which attracts you? You have now accepted a vocation as a fact in your life—*how* shall you fit your home life and your work together? Is it not a much simpler question to answer than to leave your choice of vocation to the changing fortunes of your father or your brother and always to be an accident at work rather than a girl who makes her own plans?

This may be a new idea to you. It is but one of many which you will inevitably meet in this great, changing world. Whether you will make wise use of all these new ideas will depend upon your own attitude toward life. The choice of work and the doing of work are only part of the business of living. We have to discover the power within ourselves and find out how to lay hold of it. All work, all the hours which we spend outside our work, everything that we do with other people— our home life; our good times with our friends: the parties, the picnics, the camp trips, the club meetings; the social service that we do in our own communities—everything—offers opportunity for practice in human relations. And in the practice of human relations individuality has its highest development.

Bertrand Russell has told us his conclusion that the good life is one inspired by love and guided by knowledge. By love and by knowledge we may bring in the kingdom of God. Another name for the kingdom is "the commonwealth of work."